WALKING IN CORNWALL

About the Author

Graham Uney is based near Bala in the Snowdonia National Park in Wales. Apart from writing guidebooks for Cicerone Press, he also works as a freelance journalist for a number of outdoor and wildlife magazines. This is Graham's sixth guidebook for Cicerone Press, and his 16th book to date.

Graham also runs a small outdoor activity business, Wild Walks Wales, offering holidaymakers in Snowdonia guided hill and mountain walking, wildlife walks, rock climbing and abseiling, orienteering, and wild country camping expeditions, and skills courses for walkers and mountaineers, including National Navigation Award Scheme courses, and Hill and Mountain Skills Scheme courses. He is a qualified Mountain Leader (summer and winter), and is now working towards a Mountain Instructor Award.

In his spare time Graham enjoys dog walking, rock climbing, playing the mandolin and acoustic guitar, and drinking real ale and malt whisky.

Other Cicerone guides by the author
Backpacker's Britain: Northern Scotland
Walking on the Orkney and Shetland Isles

WALKING IN CORNWALL

by Graham Uney

JUNIPER HOUSE, MURLEY MOSS,
OXENHOLME ROAD, KENDAL, CUMBRIA LA9 7RL
www.cicerone.co.uk

© Graham Uney 2015
First edition 2015
ISBN: 978 1 85284 684 8
Reprinted 2018 (with updates)
Printed by KHL Printing, Singapore

A catalogue record for this book is available from the British Library.

o⑤ Ordnance Survey® All photographs are by the author unless otherwise stated. This product includes mapping data licensed from Ordnance Survey® with the permission of the Controller of Her Majesty's Stationery Office. © Crown copyright 2015. All rights reserved. Licence number PU100012932.

Acknowledgements

Thanks to my wife Olivia for all her support during the checking of routes and writing of this book. Thanks also to Sue Viccars for her editing skills, and for supplying the photograph of Lamorna Cove at the beginning of the Land's End chapter.

Updates to this Guide

While every effort is made by our authors to ensure the accuracy of guidebooks as they go to print, changes can occur during the lifetime of an edition. Any updates that we know of for this guide will be on the Cicerone website (www.cicerone.co.uk/684/updates), so please check before planning your trip. We also advise that you check information about such things as transport, accommodation and shops locally. Even rights of way can be altered over time. We are always grateful for information about any discrepancies between a guidebook and the facts on the ground, sent by email to updates@cicerone.co.uk or by post to Cicerone, Juniper House, Murley Moss, Oxenholme Road, Kendal LA9 7RL.

Register your book: To sign up to receive free updates, special offers and GPX files where available, register your book at www.cicerone.co.uk.

Front cover: Exploring the granite outcrops on Showery Tor (Walk 6) (photo: Olivia Abbott)

CONTENTS

Route symbols on OS map extracts
(for OS legend see printed OS maps)

～～～   route   (🚶) start/finish point   ◄ route direction

Features on the overview map

────── County/Unitary
        boundary

        Urban area

～～～ National Park
        eg **DARTMOOR**

        Area of Outstanding Natural
        Beauty/National Scenic Area
        eg *Bodmin Moor*

        600m
        400m
        200m
        75m
        0m

Location of walks

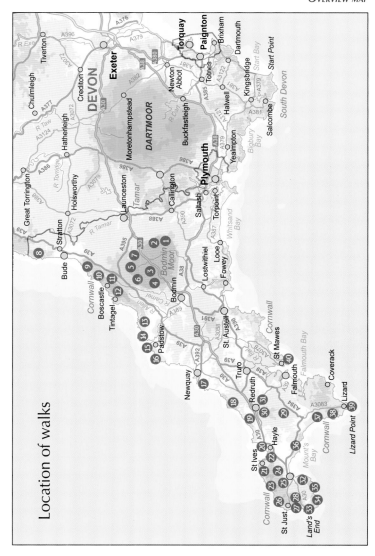

Bodmin Moor (Walks 1–7) is a real paradise for walkers who love to explore wild country

INTRODUCTION

Looking back to the lighthouse from Lizard Point (Walk 39)

The county of Cornwall is home to both the British mainland's most southwesterly point at Lands's End, and most southerly at Lizard Point. The county stretches into the Atlantic Ocean for almost 130km from its boundary with Devon, which largely follows the River Tamar, rising not far from the north coast then flowing south to reach the sea at Plymouth. Cornwall is thus almost an island, surrounded by the Celtic Sea to the north and west, the English Channel to the south, and the Tamar to the east. The Cornish display a fierce sense of independence; the name 'Kernow' ('Cornwall' in the Cornish language) is seen regularly, town and village signs appear in English and Cornish, and the black-and-white county flag is very much in evidence. Many will only know Cornwall as a holiday destination, but this is a land steeped in history and tradition with a fascinating industrial heritage.

Walking is the best way to see the county. Many places in Cornwall are only accessible on foot, and the routes described here will take you to the very best places for spectacular scenery, wildlife, prehistory, industrial archaeology, and just for relaxing and getting away from the hustle and bustle of life further east.

Being largely surrounded by water – apart from the land border with Devon – many of the walks are coastal. There are routes to stunning headlands, to some of the most important industrial sites of a long-ago age, and to some of the top places to see wildlife. Cornwall's coast is remarkably varied: the north and west coasts tend to be more rugged than the south, which is home to the sheltered wooded valleys and broad estuaries of rivers such as the Fowey, Fal and Helford.

But this guide is not all about the coast. Cornwall is also blessed in that at its heart lies one of the most exciting and scenic upland areas in England: Bodmin Moor. Here you will find wild, remote-feeling hills, many of them topped by weirdly shaped granite tors, as well as ancient settlements, burial cairns, and hill forts.

The walking in Cornwall can be surprisingly strenuous, considering that the highest hill in the whole county – Brown Willy – is only 420m above sea level. Many of the routes on Bodmin Moor lead over wild, boggy, pathless terrain; while – as anyone who's ever spent time walking around much of the UK coastline will tell you – any route along a cliff top is likely to involve a fair amount of up and down.

The 40 walks described in this book provide options suitable for all tastes and levels of ability. There are lots of short walks for Sunday strolls, and a fair few longer routes for those who want to head out for more than just a couple of hours. There is also

the opportunity for the serious walker to combine some routes for a more challenging day out (Walks 5 and 7, and 9 and 10). Note that Walks 1–7, on Bodmin Moor, are only suitable for those competent in the use of map and compass.

GEOLOGY

When most people think about which rocks make up Cornwall they immediately picture the huge granite tors that characterise many of the hilltops on Bodmin Moor. This granite sheet forms the backbone of the whole county and is by far the most important, and most obvious, rock type in Cornwall. It was formed when continental plates collided during the Late Paleozoic era 300 million years ago as part of the Cornubian batholith (the great mass of granite that intrudes throughout the southwest peninsula).

Much of the rest of the county is made up of slates from the Devonian period, but there are also outcroppings of sandstones and shales in the northeast from the Carboniferous age. The obvious exception is the peculiar rock of the Lizard peninsula. This is serpentine – a rare section of the oceanic crust which has been thrust to the surface. The only other place in the UK where serpentine is found is as far from the Lizard as it is possible to get – the island of Unst, on the northern tip of the Shetland Islands!

Since the great earth-building process, Cornwall's coastline has

Superb granite tors are a major feature of Bodmin Moor

been subjected to enormous and regular pressure from the Atlantic waves, driven onshore by the prevailing southwesterly winds. This battering has created an impressive coastline, perfect for any walking adventure. The whole array of coastal cliff formations can be seen, including zawns (small steep-sided channels), stacks, arches, caves and blowholes (where the force of the sea has caused the roof of a sea cave to collapse).

HISTORY

There is much we do not know about Cornwall's early people, but it is thought that the original settlers were probably closely linked to Neolithic peoples from Spain, Portugal and northwest France, who arrived around 3000BC. These people are credited with building the great megalithic dolmens (tombs) found in Cornwall, such as Chûn Quoit in Penwith (Walk 25). Around 2500BC the Beaker people, skilled in metalworking, reached Britain and Cornwall, and thus began the Bronze Age. A huge number of menhirs (standing stones), stone circles, barrows (burial mounds) and hut circles from this period can still be seen around Cornwall today, and many are visited on routes described in this book.

The huge tin reserves of both Cornwall and neighbouring Devon began to be exploited by man in the Bronze Age, and by about 1600BC tin from the southwest peninsula was being exported all around Europe. Since the Bronze Age, too, better tools

Chûn Castle (an Iron Age hill fort) stands on the highest part of Chûn Downs (Walk 25)

facilitated the clearing of woodland, encouraging a more settled agricultural existence.

By the start of the Iron Age, in about 750BC, the building of hill forts was common throughout Britain, and there are still many remains of these early structures around Cornwall today (Walks 14, 25 and 32). At around this time the Celts began to spread across Britain from the Continent – the language they spoke, known as Common Brittonic, evolved into several distinct tongues, including Cornish.

The Roman Conquest of Britain began in AD43, and although Cornwall was felt to be rather remote from the Roman centre of power in the southeast of the country, the road system was extended into the county. Roman milestones have been found in Cornwall: two near St Michael's Mount, two more at Tintagel, and another on Carn Brea near Redruth. Only three major Roman sites have been located in Cornwall: a fort at Calstock, another at Restormel Castle at Lostwithiel, and a third near Nanstallon.

Individual archaeological sites are detailed in the route descriptions, and there are many more to be found. Take time to study the OS map: if something appears in an antiquated font, it'll be an ancient site of some sort, and is probably well worth visiting.

INDUSTRIAL HERITAGE

You can't travel very far in Cornwall without seeing evidence of mining: the chimneys of abandoned 19th-century engine houses are visible all over the county, and some sites are thought to have been worked since the Early Bronze Age (around 2150BC). Copper and tin were the most common metals that were mined, although arsenic, silver, zinc and other metals have also been extracted commercially over the years. There are now no mines in operation in Cornwall – the last one, at South Crofty, closed in 1998 (attempts to reopen it earlier this century have so far been unsuccessful).

In Cornwall the miner goes by the local name 'Cousin Jack', (or at least the many Cornish miners who found their way oversees became known by that name). No one really knows where it originated, but some think it is because the miners were always asking for a job for their cousin Jack back home – Jack being the most popular Christian name in Cornwall at the time. There's a great song titled 'Cousin Jack' by the modern-day popular folk duo Show of Hands, who hail from Devon. The chorus goes:

Where there's a mine or a hole in the ground.
That's where I'm heading for, that's where I'm bound.
Look for me under the lode, or inside a vein.
Where the copper and clay, where the arsenic and tin,
Run in your blood they get under your skin.
I'm leaving the county behind, and I'm not coming back.
So follow me down Cousin Jack.

It is said that wherever there was a mine, anywhere in the world, a Cornishman would be working it.

WILDLIFE

Quite apart from the superb walking, for many people the main reason to visit this fabulous county is to see its amazing wildlife. The very first time I made the journey south into Cornwall I stopped the car late in the afternoon at the Levant Mines and walked down to the clifftop. A pair of choughs clacked by on the wind, and a male peregrine sat on top of the mine's chimney, glowering down at me. A great first impression!

So why all this fuss about choughs? This red-billed and red-legged member of the crow family was once common around the coasts of Britain, but by the turn of the 19th century there were only about 300

A young shelduck, recently hatched on the Hayle Estuary (Walk 20)

13

pairs left, mainly in western Scotland, Wales and the Isle of Man. The coastal grazing pastures where choughs like to feed had by and large been ploughed for arable land, and this is thought to have been one of the determining factors in the birds' decline.

The Cornish choughs fared a little better than those from the rest of England, with a few pairs continuing to nest on the seacliffs around the county. The last nesting pair was recorded in 1952, long after the bird had vanished from all other English counties. As the species became all the more rare, it became a prize target for egg collectors and trophy hunters, which only exacerbated the problem.

Then, in 2001, four wild choughs were seen in west Cornwall. Three stayed over the winter, and many people desperately hoped they would return to breed. By mid-April it was clear that two of the birds had built a nest and the female was on eggs – the first breeding choughs in England for 50 years! They can now be seen in a few coastal areas of the county, and their numbers are slowly increasing, so keep an eye out for these wonderful birds when you're on the clifftop walks in this book.

Birds can be seen everywhere in the county, from the great range of seabirds around the cliffs to the waders and wildfowl spotted on river estuaries.

Cornwall is also a hotspot for birds on migration. Being at the end of the southwest peninsula the county acts as a funnel, drawing birds along its length as they move south in the autumn, or return in the spring. Many of Cornwall's headlands are the first (or last) stopping point for birds on migration, and at the right times of year (spring and autumn), you could catch sight of all kinds of rarities.

The coastal waters too are rich in sea life, and any walk along a clifftop or beach might give you great views of common and grey seals. In the summer basking sharks may be seen too.

The county's location at the southern tip of Britain, benefiting from the warming influences of the Gulf Stream, means Cornwall has a very special flora. On the moors look for Cornish Heath (*Erica vagans*), while gorse, heather, ferns, mosses and liverworts can be found in the wetter part such as on boggy ground on Bodmin Moor. In particularly sheltered coastal locations the almost sub-tropical conditions enable palm trees to flourish, along with good showings of the ice plant (*Mesembryanthemum*): see Walk 39 for a wonderful display.

Grey seal at Porth Nanven (Walk 28)

CORNISH LANGUAGE

The Cornish language derived from the original tongue spoken by the Celtic people in the Iron Age. The mother language is known today as Common Brittonic or Old Brittonic. This ancient language evolved as the Celts moved through Britain and Western Europe and settled in different areas. By the 6th century it had split into a number of distinct variations, now known as the Brittonic languages: Cornish, Welsh, Cumbric and Breton.

Cornish, or Kernowek, has undergone something of a revival in recent times, and is considered to be a strong and important part of Cornish identity. It has recently been recognised as a minority language, and is protected as such by European Charter. In 2010 Unesco announced that its former classification of the language as 'extinct' was 'no longer accurate'.

CORNISH FARE

Ask anyone to name one product that's distinctly Cornish, and I bet the vast majority would say 'cream'. So, what's so special about Cornish cream? It is made by heating full-cream cow's milk indirectly with steam, and then leaving it in shallow pans to cool slowly. As it cools the cream rises to the surface and forms 'clots', giving us our much-loved clotted cream. In 1998 the term 'Cornish clotted cream' became a Protected Designation of Origin by European Union Directive. The milk used has to have been produced in Cornwall, and the fat content has be a minimum of 55 per cent.

There is a much disagreement between Cornishmen and Devonians about which county clotted cream originated in, and which county makes the best. On your way to Cornwall why not stop and enjoy a Devon tea, then have a Cornish one, and make your own mind up?

Few people get away with a visit to Cornwall without sampling a pasty. It is thought that the Cornish pasty can be traced back to about AD1300. The early pasties were eaten by the poorer people and were filled with potato, swede and onion. Meat was a later addition. By the 18th century the pasty was the staple diet of farmworkers and miners all over Cornwall.

GETTING THERE

Most people will drive into Cornwall, but it is also possible to get there by air, sea, train or coach.

By air

Cornwall has its own regional airport at Newquay. Flybe (tel: 0871 700 2000, www.flybe.com) operates services from Belfast, Birmingham, Edinburgh, London Gatwick, Manchester, Newcastle and Southend; easyJet (tel: 0843 104 5000, www.easyjet.com) flies from Liverpool only. German Wings (tel: 0906 294 1918, www.germanwings.com) has one flight a week from Dusseldorf (summer only).

By sea

Brittany Ferries (tel: 0871 2440744, www.brittany-ferries.co.uk) operate services from Roscoff and Santander to Plymouth, the nearest ferry port to Cornwall.

By rail

First Great Western operates services into Cornwall (tel: 0345 700 0125, www.firstgreatwestern.co.uk). For more booking options go to National Rail Enquiries (www.nationalrail.co.uk).

By coach

Truro, the county town, can be reached from London or Birmingham in about seven to eight hours by coach. Contact Traveline for booking details (see below).

By car

The most useful road access into Cornwall is the motorway, the M5, which runs southwest from the city of Bristol through the counties of Somerset and Devon to Exeter. From Exeter the A30 takes you west across the middle of Bodmin Moor, while the A38 loops south to Plymouth, then west to Bodmin where it meets the A30.

Another road route into Cornwall, especially if you are heading for the north coast, is to take the A361 from Tiverton to Barnstaple, then the A39 to Bideford and Bude, then down to Bodmin. The main road going west from Bodmin towards the Lizard, Penzance and Land's End, is the A30.

On the path along the top of Castle Point (Walk 9)

GETTING AROUND

Traveline South West gives full details of local buses and trains for getting around Cornwall (tel: 0871 200 2233, www.travelinesw.com). For driving, a good road map is essential – the main routes are highlighted above, but the county's other A roads are linked by a complex network of B and minor roads.

WHEN TO GO

Cornwall can be wonderful at any time of year. The busiest times are Easter and the months of July and August (school holidays), while Bank Holiday weekends can see endless queues of traffic heading into the peninsula too. Months worth considering are April, May, June and September for generally good, settled weather. The autumn and winter months can give truly amazing conditions too, with huge seas piling onto the cliffs, and fewer other visitors around. It can, of course, be very wet and cold too, but if you bring the right clothes this shouldn't be a problem! That said, the Gulf Stream does help to keep Cornwall milder than most other parts of Britain.

INFORMATION SOURCES

The best starting point for anyone planning a trip to Cornwall is Visit Cornwall, the official tourist board website for the county (www.visitcornwall.com). On there you'll find information on where

to go and stay, where to eat, what to do, and a wide range of other things too. There is also a section on how to get to Cornwall, as well as a complete listing of all the visitor information centres throughout the county.

Another useful website is www.cornwall-online.co.uk. For more information see Appendix B.

MAPS

The Ordnance Survey Explorer series of maps (1: 25,000) are without a doubt the best ones to buy to help you follow the walks in this book. (The map extracts that appear within the routes are taken from the 1:50,000 OS mapping blown up to 1:40,000 (2.5cm to a kilometre) for greater clarity but are intended for planning purposes only.) The sheet numbers that cover the county are: 102, 103, 104, 105, 106, 107, 108, 109, 111, 112 and 126.

The OS Landranger series are useful for planning and when travelling by car, or perhaps on a cycling tour, but their lack of fine detail can make it difficult to follow a route when walking.

USING THIS GUIDE

This guide is best used by picking a region of Cornwall to visit, perhaps finding a nice hotel, pub, guesthouse, B&B or campsite, then basing yourself there to explore all the walks within the area. As Cornwall is a relatively

Descending from Rough Tor (Walk 6)

small county, it is possible to cover a reasonable number of walks without travelling too far afield from your base. Many of the routes are short enough to do in half a day, leaving time for a visit to some of the many great tourist attractions that the county has to offer.

The 40 circular walks described are grouped into five geographical areas: Bodmin Moor, The North Coast, Penwith and West Cornwall, The Inland Mining Districts, Land's End, and The Lizard and Roseland Peninsulas. Each starts with an information panel listing start point (grid reference), distance, total ascent, time, type of terrain you will encounter, relevant map(s) to take and nearest major town. Throughout the route description features that appear on the (expanded) 1:50,000 OS map extracts shown are highlighted in bold to help you keep track of your progress.

Appendix A provides a quick-reference guide to all the routes to help you select the right one for your location, ability and timescale.

BODMIN MOOR

The Hurlers (Walk 1)

WALK 1
The Hurlers and the Cheesewring

Start/finish	Car park on the west side of Minions village (SX 259 710)
Distance	4½ miles/7.25km
Total ascent	525ft/160m
Time	2–3hrs
Terrain	Rough moorland; some boggy ground and gentle scrambling; good navigation skills essential
Map	OS Explorer 109 Bodmin Moor
Nearest town	Liskeard

This has always been one of my favourite walks on Bodmin Moor. The short stroll to the stone circles of The Hurlers is popular with tourists, but once you head away from there to the gorgeously eroded tor known as the Cheesewring, and westwards over the wild moors, you will often have the whole place to yourself.

The walk starts from the west side of the village of **Minions**. Start by heading across the moor to the northwest on the well-worn track then, after 200m, branch out northwards towards **The Hurlers**.

The standing stones of **The Hurlers** are not large, but the three separate circles arranged in a line across the moor form a unique grouping not found anywhere else in England. Local legend has it that the stones are the petrified remains of men who dared to play hurling on a Sunday.

Head west over pathless ground, aiming for an abandoned mine chimney on **Craddock Moor**. The route now takes you through some wild country as you head northwest to another stone circle. Walk across a broad ridge to explore old burial mounds above Siblyback Lake, then pick up a faint sheep track that takes you north towards the ancient field systems and settlements overlooking the buildings at Siblyback (SX 243 724).

This whole of Craddock Moor is richly blessed with signs of **Bronze Age man**. There are many burial cairns dotted around the hill, as well as an embanked avenue, a stone row consisting of 50 stones, and of course The Hurlers.

Climb gently to the northeast to reach the top of a ridge at spot height 334m. You can see that you are standing on a broad ridge running away southeast, and our walk takes us along this to the lip of an old granite quarry. Take a compass bearing to the east to cross **Witheybrook Marsh** alongside a field boundary, then continue eastwards up the (thankfully less boggy) slopes of **Stowe's Hill**. The summit is dominated by Stowe's Pound, a possible late Neolithic enclosure, and the granite tor known as **the Cheesewring**.

The Cheesewring is a strange pile of granite blocks, which appear to have been balanced very carefully one atop another. The rock formation is entirely natural and towers above Cheesewring Quarry, from where the high-grade granite was taken for building parts of The Embankment and Tower Bridge in London. Today the quarry is a rock-climbing venue.

The Cheesewring

Head to the entrance to the quarry, at its southeast corner; from here you can follow the track that was once the railway line. This goes south to a junction where you should go straight ahead, staying on the track as it bears right and passing the remains of the **South Phoenix Mine** before coming out at the road just east of Minions. Turn right along the road and walk through the village back to your car.

WALK 2

Twelve Men's Moor and Trewortha Village

Start/finish	Park sensibly on the roadside of the dead end lane running northwest along the west bank of the River Lynher from the hamlet of Berriowbridge (SX 259 761)
Distance	4 miles/6.5km
Total ascent	790ft/240m
Time	3hrs
Terrain	Pathless wild moorland, often boggy; good navigation skills essential
Map	OS Explorer 109 Bodmin Moor
Nearest town	Launceston

This walk will take you into some pretty remote country, traversing three hills around the ancient settlements of Trewortha.

Start by following a public bridleway northwards from the parking place, immediately entering open access land. Cross the first field along the bridleway, then head west gently uphill towards **Hawk's Tor**. You cross a field boundary, then climb a little more steeply to an old granite quarry just before gaining the summit rocks.

> The view to the north is one of open moorland. The distance outlines of **Brown Willy** and **Rough Tor**, the two highest hills in Cornwall, can be seen on a clear day.

Follow the ridge of Hawk's Tor southwestwards, following an old boundary down to a broad moorland col, from which it is an easy climb up onto the ridge of **Trewortha Tor**. This is a lovely ridge studded with granite tors along its length. Walk south-southwestwards, exploring as you go, then eventually drop off the west end of the ridge and down into **Trewortha Marsh**. Make for the bottom corner of the open access land, west of **King Arthur's Bed**, where a track takes you southeast to reach a public bridleway.

Walk along the bridleway to **Trewortha Farm**.

> At Trewortha Farm there is a **Bronze Age village** site. Today you'll see reconstructions of Bronze Age roundhouses; the whole area being managed as an educational resource.

Continue along the bridleway, heading east. Just 200m from the farm, as you pass back into the open access land, turn right, away from the track, and follow a compass bearing to gain the western end of the high moorland ridge of **Kilmar Tor**, right at the heart of **Twelve Men's Moor**.

> This entire area is littered with **remains of ancient man**. A glance at the map will reveal countless cairns, burial mounds, cists, hut circles and field systems. It's worth allowing extra time on a clear day to a full exploration.

Climb onto the ridge of Kilmar Tor west of High Rock, then follow the ridge northeastwards to the Ordnance Survey trig pillar at 390m. Continue in the same direction along the ridge until you are well down the eastern flank. You will pick up a track that cuts across the moor to the north, and you can follow it in that direction back to the minor road where are parked. Turn right along the lane to get back to your car.

The view of Twelve Men's Moor from the Cheesewring

WALK 3

Brown Willy from Priddacombe Downs

Start/finish	Park on the north side of the A30, opposite Jamaica Inn (SX 182 768)
Distance	6½ miles/10.5km
Total ascent	920ft/280m
Time	4hrs
Terrain	Mostly pathless and boggy moorland; good navigation skills essential
Map	OS Explorer 109 Bodmin Moor
Nearest town	Bodmin

This is quite a tough walk across one of the wildest parts of Bodmin Moor, but it does give a great route of ascent to Brown Willy, the highest hill in Cornwall.

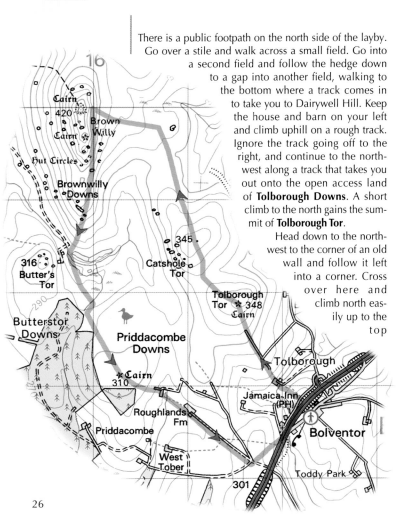

There is a public footpath on the north side of the layby. Go over a stile and walk across a small field. Go into a second field and follow the hedge down to a gap into another field, walking to the bottom where a track comes in to take you to Dairywell Hill. Keep the house and barn on your left and climb uphill on a rough track. Ignore the track going off to the right, and continue to the north-west along a track that takes you out onto the open access land of **Tolborough Downs**. A short climb to the north gains the summit of **Tolborough Tor**.

Head down to the north-west to the corner of an old wall and follow it left into a corner. Cross over here and climb north easily up to the top of **Catshole Tor**. Continue northwards along the high ground here, rather than trying to make directly for Brown Willy which can be seen across the marshy valley to the northwest. ▶

About 2km from Tolborough Tor you'll reach another boundary junction in the form of ancient wall mounds. Cross over to the northwest and climb directly to the summit cairn of **Brown Willy**, at 420m the highest point in the county.

The old Cornish name for Brown Willy is *Bronn Wennili*, which means the **Hill of the Swallows**. In 2012 a campaign was launched to have the old name resurrected in an attempt to make it sound more attractive. Local residents objected, and the *Daily Telegraph* ran a story urging campaigners to keep their 'hands off Brown Willy'!

There are two ancient cairns on the summit. The Brown Willy North Cairn sits alongside the OS trig point, and is the main top. It has never been excavated, but some suggest that it is the resting place of an ancient Cornish king.

The direct route is very wet, whereas the ridge route to the north is a little bit drier.

The summit of Brown Willy

*AONB sign on
Bodmin Moor*

Head south along the summit ridge, passing the second of the two summit cairns, then continue south as the ridge descends steeply across **Brownwilly Downs** and into the valley beyond. Here there are three small pools, and you should aim for the western side of these, picking up a track. Cross the stream via the track, but turn left immediately, following the boundary to your right as it takes you around marshy ground and out onto **Priddacombe Downs**, long been occupied by man and dotted with standing stones.

Walk over the Downs to the southeast, heading towards the large Bronze Age platform cairn at the highest point.

> **Priddacombe Downs** is now a nature reserve, owned by the Cornwall Wildlife Trust since 2001 when it was bought with funding from the Heritage Lottery Fund, English Nature, the County Environmental Trust and public donations. Although the Downs are a Site of Special Scientific Interest, they had been much degraded by overgrazing and poor management.
>
> A new grazing regime has enabled the acid grassland and valley mires to redevelop into a better wildlife habitat. Birds such as snipe, skylark, meadow pipit, stonechat, linnet and grasshopper warblers are now doing well. In some of the wetter areas purple moor grass had taken over, with a detrimental effect on the rare marsh fritillary butterfly. Winter burning and spring grazing by cattle reduces the dominance of purple moor grass, and now the marsh fritillary is on the increase.

From the cairn (SX 162 771) head just south of east on a path that leads out to a public footpath to **Priddacombe Farm**. Follow the footpath round to the right, then turn left at the farm and continue along it to **Roughlands Farm**. The onward path from the farm takes you southeast for almost 1km to a junction of paths just before the A30. Turn left here along the edge of a field with the church at

Bolventor straight ahead to find the lane that parallels to the A30, with your car parked just a short way along it. ▶

While you're here, why not pop along to Jamaica Inn for a celebratory bar meal and a drink.

Jamaica Inn was built as a coaching inn on the old turnpike between Launceston and Bodmin in 1750. It is thought that half of the brandy and a quarter of all the tea being smuggled into Britain back then was brought in via the coasts of Cornwall and Devon, and much of it was hidden here; the inn's wild and remote location made it ideal for this purpose.

Jamaica Inn is also famous as being at the heart of the Daphne du Maurier novel of the same name. It was her first commercial success, and was turned into a film, directed by Alfred Hitchcock and staring Charles Laughton and Maureen O'Hara. Du Maurier wrote 38 books in total, and died in 1989. The current owners of Jamaica Inn have created a memorial room to her.

WALK 4

Brown Willy from Garrow Downs

Start/finish	Park off the narrow lane, making sure you are not blocking access to buildings or gateways at Candra Farm, at the foot of Casehill Downs (SX 117 779)
Distance	7½ miles/12km
Total ascent	1070ft/325m
Time	5hrs
Terrain	Pathless and boggy moorland; good navigation skills essential
Map	OS Explorer 109 Bodmin Moor
Nearest town	Bodmin

This is quite a long approach to Brown Willy but it takes in some hidden gems along the way, and is a good route for those wanting to get off the beaten track.

Start by walking east along the lane through **Candra** to reach a gateway to **Casehill**, by a well. Once through the gate, the lane becomes a track and swings off to the house on the left. Go straight ahead following the boundary to the right to pick up a public footpath that goes east to **King Arthur's Hall**.

King Arthur's Hall is a late Neolithic/early Bronze Age ceremonial site. It consists of 56 stones arranged in a rectangle with an earthwork running around them. Cattle have damaged it in the past, and a gated fence now keeps livestock out. Its actual use is not known for sure, but a similar site in Brittany was definitely a Bronze Age cremation site. It is reminiscent of Staneydale Temple in the Shetland Islands, also with an unconfirmed purpose.

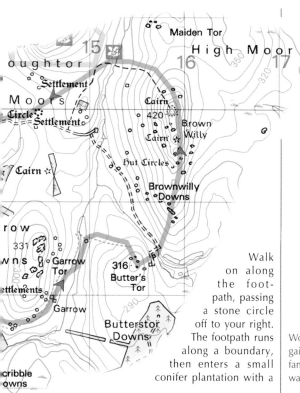

Walk on along the footpath, passing a stone circle off to your right. The footpath runs along a boundary, then enters a small conifer plantation with a

Worth a detour to gain its top if you fancy a slightly longer walk.

stream, a tributary of the De Lank River. Cross the stream and leave the wood, continuing along the footpath as it takes you around the south side of Garrow Tor. ▶

Continue along the public footpath as it passes through an amazing area

The view through to Garrow Downs

The head of the De Lank River with Brown Willy rising above it

of ancient field systems and settlements at **Garrow**. The route leads around to the east side of Garrow Tor where you cross another tributary of the De Lank River. Here you should head east, to where the path becomes very vague. Re-enter open access land on **Butter Tor**, then turn south to gain the top of this little hill at 316m (SX 154 782).

To the east is a valley containing three pools. Head directly downhill to the left side of these and you'll pick up a track. Follow the track across the stream, then climb just east of north up the broad, rough ridge of **Brownwilly Downs**. This a superb route, taking you directly to the south cairn on the main Brown Willy ridge, and just beyond this the main top with its large ancient cairn and Ordnance Survey trig point.

> To the northwest is **Rough Tor**, the second-highest hill in Cornwall (see Walk 6), while the valley that lies between is full of ancient field systems and settlements. This is a fascinating area to explore, especially on a sunny day.

From the summit of **Brown Willy** head northwest down into the valley, and cross the De Lank River again. Walk west around an old boundary wall and make for the largest area of field systems due south of the summit of Rough Tor. Keep on the south side of this old village site, and follow a compass bearing south-west to a stone circle. Just beyond this there is a track that continues in the same southwest line, along the southern slopes of **Louden Hill**. Follow this track right through to **Candra Hill** and **Middle Moor Cross**.

> **Middle Moor Cross** is a scheduled monument. It is a medieval wayside cross, set within a trackway that gives access onto these western fringes of Bodmin Moor. It is a 2m-high granite upright set into a large granite slab. It also goes by the name Mid Moor Post, and early records confirm that it is in its original position. The cross is incised into the granite, and the style indicates that it is probably of very early medieval date.

To the south of the cross is **Camperdown Farm**. Continue southwest along what is now more of a lane than a track until the boundary on your left ends and you can walk off left across the moor to the top of **Alex Tor** at 291m. Head south from the summit to find Candra where your car is parked.

WALK 5
*Brown Willy and the
source of the River Fowey*

Start/finish	Park by the Penpont Water just south of Bowithick hamlet (SX 183 826)
Distance	5¾ miles/9.25km
Total ascent	850ft/260m
Time	3.5hrs
Terrain	Rough pathless moorland, very boggy in places; good navigation skills essential
Map	OS Explorer 109 Bodmin Moor
Nearest town	Camelford

This walk is ideal for those who really want to get into the wildest parts of Bodmin Moor. Note that the route is pathless throughout, and so is only really suitable for those who know how to take and follow compass bearings.

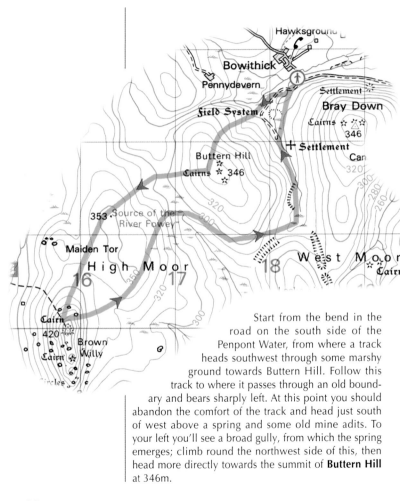

Start from the bend in the road on the south side of the Penpont Water, from where a track heads southwest through some marshy ground towards Buttern Hill. Follow this track to where it passes through an old boundary and bears sharply left. At this point you should abandon the comfort of the track and head just south of west above a spring and some old mine adits. To your left you'll see a broad gully, from which the spring emerges; climb round the northwest side of this, then head more directly towards the summit of **Buttern Hill** at 346m.

Brown Willy's summit ridge from the approach over High Moor

▶ To continue westwards to Brown Willy and the source of the Fowey is to get further into the wildest parts of the moor. If the ground underfoot is reasonably dry, and your navigation skills are up to the task, soak up the views from Buttern Hill then head west down to a broad (and occasionally damp) col at spot height 298m (SX 168 815).

The ground rises to the southwest in a gentle gradient, and you should aim for the cairns on **High Moor** at 354m, then descend just 12m (in altitude) to the southwest to gain the northern slopes of Brown Willy. Climb steeply but easily up the north ridge of **Brown Willy** to the summit cairn and triangulation pillar.

The route on from the summit lies to the east. ▶ Take a bearing down to **Fowey Well**, and then follow a compass bearing to the northeast across the moor to the source of the River Fowey.

The **Upper Fowey** is a Site of Special Scientific Interest for its wet heath vegetation and herbaceous valley mires. Plants to look out for here are sundews and butterworts, both of which are fascinating to find and thrive in very poor soils. Plants that do well in our uplands have evolved to cope with the typically acidic, nutrient-poor soils, so that for the most part only those species that can tolerate these conditions

If you're finding the going wet and difficult at this stage, it is probably wise to turn back.

You may want to divert from the route slightly to explore the summit ridge to the south, and the second ancient cairn.

live there. The exceptions are sundews and butter-worts, which take their nutrients from insects. They catch tiny insects on their leaves by attracting them with a sweet, sticky substance. Once the insect is caught, the plant slowly devours it.

As you approach the source of the Fowey, predictably the ground is going to get a bit wetter. Pick a careful way through the bog and you'll find a little pool, seemingly among many others, where this major Cornish river begins its life. Cross to the east side of the valley, and walk around the southern slopes of **Buttern Hill** (or climb back over the hill if you prefer). Once you have made it safely around to the east side of Buttern Hill walk north down the broad valley that lies between Buttern Hill to the west and **Bray Down** to the east (see Walk 11). At the bottom of the valley you will reach the road where your car is parked.

WALK 6
Rough Tor and Brown Willy from the north

Start/finish	From the A39 at the northeast end of Camelford turn southeast to Tregoodwell along Roughtor Road to a large car park at its end (SX 137 819)
Distance	4 miles/6.5km
Total ascent	1095ft/335m
Time	3hrs
Terrain	Pathless moorland, boggy in places; rocky scrambling on Rough Tor; good navigation skills essential
Map	OS Explorer 109 Bodmin Moor
Nearest town	Camelford

This is a great walk on the northern fringe of Bodmin Moor, taking in the two highest hills of Cornwall. Rough Tor is a popular place with walkers, giving an easy ascent to the granite tors that adorn the summit ridge. Not many people continue on to Brown Willy from here, giving you the feeling that you're really getting away from it all.

Start by heading to the bridge over the river, just down from the car park. This leads out onto the open access land of Rough Tor (pronounced 'Rowter').

Little Rough Tor and Rough Tor from Showery Tor

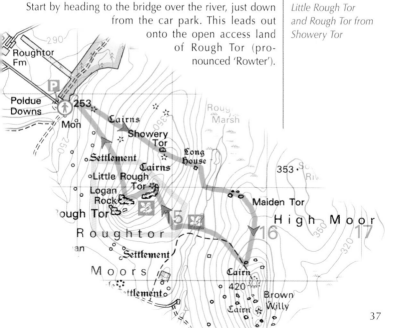

Walking towards Rough Tor from Little Rough Tor

There is no need to worry about walking off paths and tracks as a notice in the car park requests that you avoid the **well-trodden paths** to control erosion, and explore as much as you can away from the main routes.

At the northeastern end of the Rough Tor ridge you can see an obvious pile of granite rocks, known as **Showery Tor**. Make for this, walking easily over short-cropped grass to gain the delightful little summit. ◀

The ridge leading southwest to Rough Tor is tempting… Shorten the walk if you like, but why would you when the wonderful tors of Brown Willy lie just across the valley to the southeast?

From Showery Tor head southeast down to the site of an old long house. The valley ahead is very wet – this is where the De Lank River rises at **Roughtor Marsh**. From the long house head just east of south towards the corner of an old stone bank. Now turn east and climb up to the summit of **Maiden Tor** at 342m (SX 158 808). **Brown Willy** rises just to the south now and it is an easy walk to gain its summit at 420m.

To get back to Rough Tor head northwest to pick up a vague path and follow it down to cross the De Lank River. The path bends around to the west here, but you should leave it and follow a compass bearing directly for the tors on **Little Rough Tor**. A cairn marks the top of this intermediate hill at 390m. The granite tors all along the ridge here are wonderful, typical rounded slabs of the roughest rock, in many cases piled one on top of another and looking very unstable.

Continue along the ridge, more to the southwest now, to the main summit of **Rough Tor** with its war memorial. To the west of the summit iis a superb granite block, fashioned by the wind and rain into a huge arm-chair. An easy short scramble leads to the top for a seat with a spectacular view.

To the north of Rough Tor the slopes are bouldery, but you can pick a careful way down through the rocks, aiming northwest for the car park which lies just over 1km away over the moor.

WALK 7
Bray Down and Leskernick Hill

Start/finish	Park on the roadside on the lane between Bowithick and Trebray (SX 191 826)
Distance	5 miles/8km
Total ascent	630ft/190m
Time	3hrs
Terrain	Pathless moorland, boggy in places; careful navigation required
Map	OS Explorer 109 Bodmin Moor
Nearest town	Camelford

A short walk, but a fine introduction to Bodmin Moor: walking in a wild moorland setting, yet never too far away from the minor roads that traverse the moor's northeast corner. It can feel very desolate up here, however, but if the mists do roll in and you start to feel lost, just head northeast and you'll soon hit one of these minor roads.

Two thirds of the route is over pathless terrain, with the final third being an easy stroll along a quiet lane.

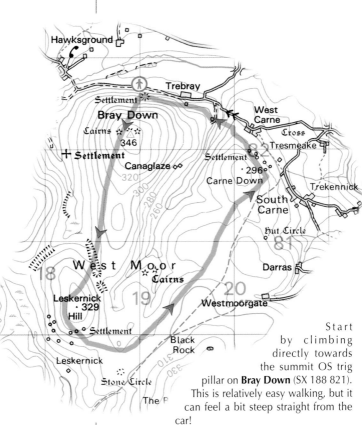

Start by climbing directly towards the summit OS trig pillar on **Bray Down** (SX 188 821). This is relatively easy walking, but it can feel a bit steep straight from the car!

The valley to the east holds a stream that drains from a spring below Leskernick Hill. Our route keeps to the high ground around this valley. Continue by following the broad ridge to the west of south, aiming for the distant col just before the rise up to the summit of **Leskernick Hill**. The final climb to the top is short, and you are greeted by an ancient cairn. On the south side of the hill there are some amazing examples of settlements,

a stone circle, a stone row and a cist – all well worth exploring.

Bray Down from across High Moor

Leskernick is a well-preserved Bronze Age settlement, with at least 50 round houses set within a huge field system. University College London has been running archaeological and geological projects here since 1995. The surface boulders are known as 'clitter', found throughout Devon and Cornwall where granite outcrops. The surrounding moorland is relatively free of rocks, and there are no tors on Leskernick Hill, so the scattered hilltop boulders are associated with transitional phases on the fringes of glaciated areas.

Walk south to see the settlement, then head across to the stone circle (SX 185 799). Walk east to the stone row, then continue east for 300m to where a junction of bridleways is shown on the OS map. ▶

Don't expect to see very much here: many of the public rights of way over Bodmin Moor simply indicate an ancient right to cross the moor, rather than suggesting that there will be a path on the ground!

41

A track cuts over West Moor a little further north, if you want to gain that for the security of having something more definite underfoot.

Walk on a compass bearing to the northeast, over **West Moor**. ◄ Aim for **Carne Down**, and the point where the track and public bridleway meet (SX 202 814). Follow the track northeastwards out to the minor lane between South Carne and West Carne. At the point where you meet the lane, take the public footpath to your left, heading through fields to the northwest to **West Carne**. In West Carne you'll meet the lane again, having just cut off a big corner. Turn left and follow the lane back to your car, ignoring the turn off to the right just before **Trebray**.

THE NORTH COAST

Climbing to Com Head (Walk 14)

WALK 8
Sharpnose Point from Coombe

Start/finish	Duckpool Beach, Coombe: small car park overlooking the bay, toilets (SS 201 116)
Distance	7 miles/11.25km
Total ascent	1700ft/520m
Time	4hrs
Terrain	Coastal walking along high cliffs; return through fields and woodland, muddy in places
Map	OS Explorer 126 Clovelly & Hartland
Nearest town	Bude

This is a lovely walk in a very dramatic setting, leading you to the most northerly parish in Cornwall.

Striding out along the top of Steeple Point

Start by following the coast path signs from the car park, climbing quite steeply at first northwestwards to the top of

Steeple Point. Here great shelves of rock fall away to Wren Beach while breakers pile against the tiny offshore Kempthorn's Rock, Pigsback Rock and Squench Rock. It is possible to get down to the beach, and the OS map shows a public footpath, but the way is now blocked by a rock fall, and the route is not easy.

Our walk stays above the beach and leads along the clifftop to the next big headland, **Lower Sharpnose Point**. The radio masts at Harscott High Cliff, just inland from Lower Sharpnose Point, are part of a GCHQ communication network.

As you near Lower Sharpnose Point you get a view along the next section of coastline, across Holacombe Beach to Rane Point, splitting two lovely sandy beaches: Rane Beach to the south and Stanbury Beach to the north. The route from Lower Sharpnose Point goes east, inland towards the radio masts, then leads northwards to regain the clifftop path.

The way passes high above Rane Point, then continues northwards around Stanbury Point above Hippa Rock. Continue northwards above Greenway Beach, getting closer to Higher Sharpnose Point all the while. In common with much of the north Cornish coastal path there is a fair amount of ascent and descent on this section, but you'll soon find yourself at Higher Sharpnose.

Beyond **Higher Sharpnose Point** the way drops into the deep valley of **Tidna Shute**. Ignore the public footpath that head off eastwards along the Shute, and climb out northwards, still on the coastal path.

Ignore the next public footpath on the right, and just beyond this junction you'll come to Hawker's Hut, just to the left of the coast path.

The **Reverend Robert Stephen Hawker** was both a parson and poet. He was vicar of Morwenstow parish – the most northerly in Cornwall – from 1834 to 1874. Hawker made it his duty to care for the victims of shipwrecks on the wild Morwenstow coast, and to find and bury the dead.

Just beyond Hawker's Hut you'll reach a footpath junction. Leave the coastal path now and head eastwards along the public footpath into Morwenstow, passing the church as you enter the village.

From the church walk along the lane to reach The Bush Inn. Turn right at the inn onto a public footpath.

This takes you south into the head of Tidna Shute, then up through fields to the old farmstead at **Tonacombe**. Keep the farm to your left and continue south out to a minor lane at **Stanbury**. Go left along the lane at Stanbury, then take another public footpath on the right through the farm. This will take you down to cross a little spring, then southeast across two fields to another lane. ▸

However, our route crosses the lane to **Eastaway Manor**; keep to the left of the buildings along the drive, then after 200m cross a little stream. The footpath now climbs uphill out of the valley and on towards the village of **Woodford**.

As you approach Woodford you'll come to a footpath junction. Turn right here along a green lane, and then left along the road in Woodford. In 50m turn right again onto a public footpath. This takes you slightly uphill, then down into the valley of Woodford Wood. Take a right down to cross the stream of Mill Leat, then follow the obvious footpath along the south side of the stream to emerge on a lane just outside of **Coombe**. Go right along the lane, and follow it down into the bottom of the valley. Here you'll come to a road junction from where you earlier accessed Duckpool. Turn right here and follow the lane back to the car park.

For a quick return to Coombe you can turn right and just follow this lane.

WALK 9
Crackington Haven to Dizzard Point

Start/finish	Crackington Haven: pay and display car park, toilets, pub, cafés (SX 143 967)
Distance	7¼ miles/11.75km
Total ascent	2030ft/620m
Time	4–5hrs
Terrain	Coastal walking along high cliffs; return through fields and quiet country lanes
Map	OS Explorer 111 Bude, Boscastle & Tintagel
Nearest town	Bude

A fine yet surprisingly taxing coastal walk northwards from Crackington Haven, giving superb views. The route back is through farmland and takes you to the delightful parish church of St Gennys.

Start by walking to the bridge at the entrance to the car park. Turn right and follow the road up and around the sharp bend to the right. Just over 100m later you'll come to the coast path on the left. Follow this as it climbs steeply up out of the haven. The path gains a headland above Black Rock, and you should follow a fence overlooking the cliffs, ignoring the obvious path that goes eastwards through a field on the ridgetop.

Stay on the path closest to the coast, and it soon takes you down through flower-filled slopes to a little wooden footbridge over a stream. The steep path climbing out of the other side leads quickly to Castle Point for a magnificent view to the northeast along the coastal cliffs.

The narrow ridge of Castle Point is a delight to walk, and the way is obvious as you head first east into a little col, then northeastwards above the flat rocks of **Cleave Strand**.

The view to Pencarrow Point from Crackington Haven

There is a lot of 'upping and downing' along this bit of coast, and the route dips into two deep gullies before reaching **Chipman Point**. Ahead now, along the shoreline far below, you can see **Dizzard Point**, and our route follows the clifftop path all the way to the OS triangulation pillar that stands above.

Just beyond the trig point drop downhill to a fence. Turn right here along a public footpath and follow it round the field edge to the farm at East Dizzard. Go south out of the farmyard along the lane to meet the public road at spot height 149 (SX 168 985). Now walk south along the quiet public lane, passing Dizzard Farm, Old Dizzard and **Whitemoor**. Just beyond Whitemoor you'll come to a junction just before a telephone box. Turn right here and follow the lane westwards to **Higher Tresmorn**, then on to **Lower Tresmorn** and Cleave.

As you approach **Cleave** the lane swings to the left. Go around this bend, then as it turns back to the right by the farm buildings, there is a public footpath sign to the left. Follow the path through a little wood, then steeply downhill to cross a stream. A steep climb out of the opposite side leads to a field. Bear left here, and you'll pick up a footpath that takes you around field edges to **St Gennys**.

Once on the public lane in St Gennys turn right, and walk for 50m towards the end of the lane. Before you reach the end, by the church, look for a public footpath on the left. ◄ It leads up a short bank via a few wooden steps (sometimes a little overgrown during the summer months) into a large field. Turn right and follow the field edge westwards, now well signposted, towards the coast. You'll soon pass through a gate, and will find yourself on the headland above Black Rock. Turn left on the coast path, and retrace your steps down the steep hill into **Crackington Haven**.

Take a look at the Norman church, dedicated to St Genesius and enjoying what must be one of the most stunning locations in the country.

WALK 10

The Strangles and Cambeak

Start/finish	Crackington Haven: pay and display car park, toilets, pub, cafés (SX 143 967)
Distance	5 miles/8km
Total ascent	1530ft/465m
Time	3–4hrs
Terrain	High coastal cliffs; rough and rocky descent to The Strangles; return via woodland gorge, often muddy
Map	OS Explorer 111 Bude, Boscastle & Tintagel
Note	At the time of writing the public footpath down to the beach was inaccessible due to storm damage; the National Trust had warning signs in place.
Nearest town	Bude

A popular walk south along the coast from Crackington Haven. The cliff scenery at The Strangles is among the best in Cornwall, while the route back takes you through a lovely wooded valley.

From the car park in Crackington Haven head out to the little road bridge, then go left and down to the shore. The South West Coast Path leads around the cliffs to **Bray's Point**, then climbs high above the bay of **Tremoutha Haven**. Look for the gorgeous little waterfalls here that tumble down the cliffs onto the shore.

The rock formations around Crackington Haven and south to The Strangles are important for geologists. The rocks are over 300 million years old; on view are contorted under-cliffs where the softer layers of rock have slumped, forming a series of fissures. Crackington Haven has given its name to a geological phe-nomenon, the

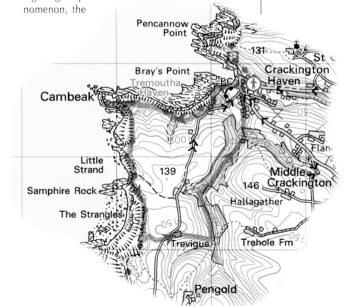

Crackington Formation, a fractured shale that has been metamorphosed by intense volcanic heat and pressure. Even the name 'Crackington' comes from a Cornish word for sandstone, *crak*.

As you approach the first big headland beyond Tremoutha Haven, **Cambeak**, the route dips into a gully known as Cam Draught. The climb out is steep, but you'll soon find yourself on the amazing headland of Cambeak. The views back towards Crackington Haven are stunning, while those stretching southwards towards The Strangles are among the finest in Cornwall.

Head south along the clifftop path, admiring the views down to the beach – **Little Strand** – as you go.

Looking back you might be able to pick out the rock arch known as the **Northern Door**. It is quite low, but the rock formations that make up the arch are incredible.

The view along the coast southwards from The Strangles

Beyond Little Strand you come to the main beach at **The Strangles**. The path down to the beach from the clifftop may be passable (see Note above), and if so the coast here is well worth exploring at shore level.

The route back to Crackington Haven leaves the coast above The Strangles and takes you inland to a public road. Turn left along the lane, then right as you go past the farm at **Trevigue**.

The National Trust owns the farm at **Trevigue**, and has tenant farmers managing it. The present building dates from the 16th century, although there has been a farm here since the Norman Conquest.

From Trevigue head east along the public footpath, crossing a couple of fields as you descend into a wooded valley. Don't go all the way down to the stream; look for a public footpath junction just above it, and turn left here. Follow the footpath along the west side of the stream, through the woods, for just over 1km. At this point the footpath crosses the stream via a small footbridge, then goes around a little spur to cross a second stream via another bridge. A popular public footpath now takes you northwards back into Crackington Haven for a well-earned pint.

WALK 11
Boscastle

Start/finish	Boscastle: large pay and display car park opposite the Cobweb Inn, cafes, toilets (SX 099 912)
Distance	3½ miles/5.5km
Total ascent	1215ft/370m
Time	2hrs
Terrain	Village footpaths and coastal path along high cliffs
Map	OS Explorer 111 Bude, Boscastle & Tintagel
Note	This walk takes you on a figure-of-eight around the headlands on both sides of the harbour. It can easily be split to make two shorter walks if desired.
Nearest town	Camelford

A popular short walk around the harbour at Boscastle. The route takes in the delightful picture-book village as well as the adjacent coastal headlands. You'll get to see the old lookout station on the dramatic headland at Willapark, as well as the historic farming strips of Forrabury Stitches.

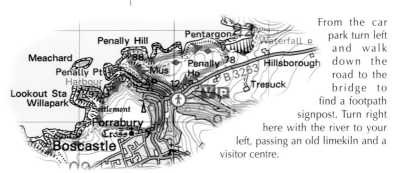

From the car park turn left and walk down the road to the bridge to find a footpath signpost. Turn right here with the river to your left, passing an old limekiln and a visitor centre.

The kiln was used in the 18th century to convert imported limestone into quicklime which the villagers used to reduce the acidity of the soil in their fields, as well as for whitewashing their cottages.

A little further on is the Witchcraft Museum – 50 years old and believed to be the biggest of its kind in the world – and then the YHA building. Go between these two and follow the lane up above the north side of the harbour.

The walk passes below a row of house, then takes you out to **Penally Point** right at the entrance of Boscastle Harbour.

The natural harbour of Boscastle is believed to have been used by man since 2000BC. This tiny village hit the news headlines in 2004 when a flash flood washed 75 cars, 5 caravans, and 6 buildings into the sea. Approximately 100 homes and businesses were destroyed, and a fleet of Sea King rescue helicopters were brought in to pluck about 150 people off rooftops and out of trees. There were no major injuries, and thankfully no loss of life.

From Penally Point walk eastwards along the coast path, climbing to the top of **Penally Hill**. The route drops into a little col, then climbs uphill again. Go over two low hills, with a little dip between them, then look for a public footpath on the right as you approach **Pentargon**. Turn right away from the coast and follow the path to the B3263. Turn right and pick up a permissive footpath that runs parallel to the road, along its north side. This soon becomes a public right of way as you pass **Penally House**, leading back to the centre of Boscastle.

To walk the southern half of the figure-of-eight circuit return to the bridge, but instead of taking the path on the north side of the Valency River, cross the bridge and turn right along the south side of the harbour. The coast path soon starts to climb, gaining height steadily above the harbour.

As you continue around the headland you'll see the lookout station on the hill known as Willapark. There are two sea inlets that almost, but not quite, separate Willapark from the mainland: the first you'll come to is Eastern Blackapit, with Western Blackapit being a little further along. The narrow neck of land between the two gives access onto **Willapark** itself.

The natural harbour at Boscastle

The **coastguard lookout** on Willapark was built in the 19th century by a local merchant. He had it built as his summerhouse, but it wasn't long before the Board of Trade leased it from him and used it as a lookout for their excisemen in an attempt to prevent smuggling. After this period it became a proper coastguard station, and remained so into the 1970s when the National Trust took it on. Today the lookout is leased to the National Coastwatch Institute and run as a voluntary station.

Once you've explored Willapark, make your way back across the neck of land, and turn right along the clifftop path, looking down into the depths of Western Blackapit.

SHIPWRECKS

Western Blackapit has seen its fair share of shipwrecks. In January 1843 the cargo ship *Jessie Logan* ran aground en route from Calcutta to Liverpool. All the crew perished, and much of her cargo came ashore, including bags of rice, sugar and cotton. A fist and cutlass fight between the customs officers and locals ensued; the two ringleaders were prosecuted and received 12 months' hard labour for 'feloniously plundering and stealing from a ship'.

In December 1884 the steam-powered freighter *Alliance* disappeared en route from Cardiff to St Nazaire with a cargo of Welsh coal. It was initially thought that the coal had produced methane in the very wet conditions, and that the ship had exploded. However, a report from Cardiff stated that she was in good seaworthy condition when she left port, and that she was very well ventilated. The crew of 16 perished, and debris from the wreck was found washed up at Western Blackapit.

The ground to your left as you walk along the coast path is **Forrabury Common**, also known as 'The Stitches'. Turn left along a public footpath and head towards the church alongside the common.

Forrabury Common is divided into 42 plots known locally as 'Stitches'. This was a form of land tenure in medieval times, called 'stitch meal'. The land was cultivated in long plots, each growing a different crop, and each separated from the next stitch by a narrow grass sward. In the winter months the Common is grazed, and the Stitches are not so easy to see.

Turn right into the churchyard of St Symphorian's. At the eastern corner pick up a public footpath heading east to the lower corner of the Stitches. Turn right and head down to New Road. Cross straight over, and pick up a small lane known as Old Road. Turn left and walk down the hill to the bridge at the centre of lower Boscastle.

WALK 12
Tintagel and Willapark

Start/finish	Tintagel Visitor Centre: pay and display car park, toilets, cafés, pubs (SX 058 883)
Distance	3¾ miles/6km
Total ascent	930ft/285m
Time	2–3hrs
Terrain	Town lanes and coastal footpath along high cliffs
Map	OS Explorer 111 Bude, Boscastle & Tintagel
Nearest town	Camelford

A very popular location, and rightly so. The walk takes in the ancient settlement on the headland at Willapark, as well as the world-famous Tintagel Castle, famous for its links with the legendary King Arthur.

Turn right out of the car park and follow the B3263 eastwards for about 1.5km, until you come to a radio mast on the left. Here you'll see a public footpath on the left heading for the coast. The route leads downhill to a gully, below which is one of the loveliest beaches on this stretch of coastline, **Bossiney Haven**.

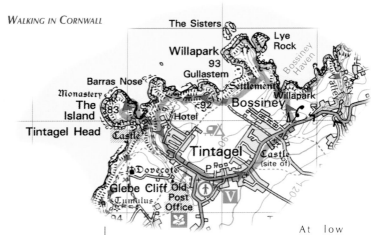

At low tide you can walk around the little rocky headland that separates Bossiney Haven from the next beach to the east, **Benoath Cove**. However, be especially aware of the tides here, as at high tide the beaches are almost completed covered by the sea.

The massive headland to the northwest of Bossiney Haven is Willapark (not the same one as stands above Boscastle!). Once you've enjoyed the lovely white sands of the beach, regain the clifftop and walk along the South West Coast Path to the northwest, and out to explore **Willapark**. The rocks offshore are known as The Sisters.

On the Willapark headland are the remains of an **Iron Age settlement**. These can be hard to see, but if you look closely you'll find the odd broken remains of banks and ditches.

Return to the main clifftop and turn right, following the coastal path around the top of Smith's Cliff to the next big headland, Barras Nose. ◀

Keep an eye on the beaches below the cliffs, and also out in the surf, as grey seals are often seen here.

Continue onto **Barras Nose**; there are superb views westwards towards Tintagel Castle, and also along the coast eastwards to Boscastle.

58

Barras Nose was the first coastal property to be bought by the National Trust. The North Cornwall Railway came to Camelford in 1893, bringing large numbers of tourists on the trail of the Arthurian Legends. The large hotel above Barras Nose was built, advertising itself as being on the spot where Tennyson gained inspiration for his 'Idylls of the King'. The locals became concerned that tourism was taking over, and opposed any further developments. In 1896 the princely sum of £505 was raised to buy 15 acres of the surrounding clifftop, and in 1897 this became the Trust's first English coastal property.

And now for the chief attraction at Tintagel: the **Castle**. From Barras Nose follow the coast path across the cliffs and down to Tintagel Haven. Here you'll probably be confronted by a couple of hundred tourists, all here to see the home of legendary historical figure King Arthur.

The view over to Tintagel Castle

Whether you buy into the Arthurian legends or not, the castle is well worth a visit, despite the fact that it is very much in ruins. A path leads up to the entrance gate (English Heritage entrance fees apply).

Tintagel Castle was built in the 13th century by Earl Richard of Cornwall, and stands on the site of a Celtic fortress. It was Geoffrey of Monmouth who claimed that the earlier castle was the one-time home of Igraine, mother of the legendary King Arthur.

When you've finished marvelling at Tintagel Castle head back out of the gate and pick up the path that starts tight under a big rocky headland. This overlooks the lane that goes down to the Haven. Follow the path to a small car park (usually a burger van here too), then up a short leafy lane to the main street through the village. There are plenty of cafes and pubs here, as well as the usual tourist tat shops. Worthy of note is the Old Post Office (National Trust), originally a traditional longhouse and at least 600 years old. Continue along the main street back to your car.

WALK 13
Around Port Isaac Bay

Start/finish	Pay and display car park on New Road in Port Isaac: toilets (SW 999 809)
Distance	4 miles/6.5km
Total ascent	980ft/300m
Time	2–3hrs
Terrain	Farmland paths, often muddy; return along clifftops
Map	OS Explorer 106 Newquay & Padstow and 111 Bude, Boscastle & Tintagel
Nearest town	Padstow

A nicely varied walk giving you a sample of the delightful coast at Port Isaac, as well as a chance to discover the quiet paths and tracks inland from the village.

From the seaward side of the car park turn left along the coastal path (your views to the right are towards the lovely Port Gaverne). Follow the path around the headland, marvelling at the views out to sea, and into the next cove along to the west, **The Haven**. This is where you enter **Port Isaac** proper; emerge onto Fore Street, and head downhill.

> **Port Isaac** was a very busy port from the Middle Ages right up to the mid-19th century. Coal, timber, pottery and stone were among the regular cargoes coming and going from the town. Today the age-old occupation of fishing is still important, but tourism plays a hugely important role too.

The area around The Haven and Fore Street is very picturesque, and you should aim to at least stop at a café for a cream tea, and to take in the views.

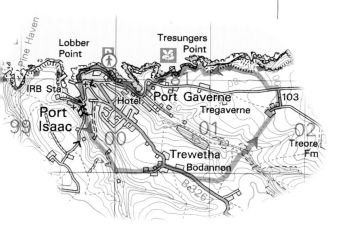

Port Isaac is also becoming increasingly well known for its role as a **TV and film set**: the comedy drama series *Doc Martin* is filmed here. Those familiar with the UK folk music scene will probably have heard of the shanty singers Fisherman's Friends who hail from the village and who have been doing the rounds of folk festivals for the last 15 years or so.

Walk round the corner by the Golden Lion. Ignore the turn on the left into Middle Street, but take the next left up Church Hill. Just over 100m up the hill you'll come to a public footpath on the left, as the road swings to the right. Follow the footpath down into the valley, and above a small water treatment works. You'll soon come to a house. Go right along the driveway, then take the public footpath to the left again. This bends round to the left and down to a footbridge. Cross this and climb steeply eastwards along the path to **Trewetha**.

You'll come out onto the B3267; turn right along the road for just under 400m. A public footpath on the left cuts over a field to the east, joining another footpath

Walking near Trewethart above Port Gaverne

where you turn left again to walk around the head of a little valley. Go through a gate, then walk northeast down into a deeper valley and cross a stream. The path continues heading northeast as you climb up to the farm at Trewethart. Keep the main farm buildings to your right and head along the drive to pick up a minor road. Turn left and walk to a T-junction with another minor road. Turn left along this for 100m, and look for a public footpath on the right that takes you down a little valley to the coast. Turn left on the coast path; this will lead you into **Port Gaverne**, from where the road is followed back to your car.

WALK 14
Pentire Point

Start/finish	Park at the old lead mines just beyond Pentireglaze, New Polzeath (SW 940 799)
Distance	3¾ miles/6km
Total ascent	875ft/265m
Time	2–3hrs
Terrain	Coastal path along high cliffs
Map	OS Explorer 106 Newquay & Padstow
Nearest town	Padstow

This is one of those walks that turns out to be better than anticipated. The headland looks low at first sight, but almost as soon as you leave the lead mines you're confronted with magnificent cliffs and expansive views along the coast.

Start by heading east through the gate at the top of the car park. This leads by the old lead mines and out to a gate overlooking Pengirt Cove. The Pentireglaze lead mines operated from 1580 through to 1883, and you can still see the remains of the old waste tips as you head out to the coast.

Turn left on the South West Coast Path above Pengirt Cove and head towards **Com Head** along the clifftop. It's a popular stretch of coastline, so expect to greet lots of other people. Beyond Com Head look down to the beaches on your right. There are lovely little secluded coves here, and if you're lucky you might see some grey seals hauled out.

Off shore the little island of The Mouls adds drama to the scene, and as you climb up a little grassy path at the top end of Sandinway Beach you'll get a particularly fine view of it. Beyond Sandinway Beach the path splits. You can go left to cut out a walk around the headland of The Rumps, but it would be a shame to miss it, so go straight on down to a little col by an old stone wall.

The Rumps are twin grassy knolls, each with an obvious path leading to the top. Enjoy the short stroll around this ancient hill fort, then return to the main path and walk westwards up through a little rocky gully. After 200m there is a path junction, with a footpath heading off inland alongside a hedge and fence. ◀ The walk continues along the clifftop to **Pentire Point**, from where views stretch way out across Padstow Bay to distant Trevose Head.

From Pentire Point our route heads southeastwards along the cliff, rather than running along its top. The way

This can be taken as a short cut back to Pentire Farm, then along the drive to the lead mines car park.

*On the path around
Pentire Point*

is very obvious and soon leads into a deep gully. A climb up the other side gains another smaller headland overlooking the northern end of Hayle Bay.

Follow the upper path into the head of another gully. This leads inland, initially to the north, then around to **Pentire Farm**. Turn right at Pentire Farm and follow the drive back to your car.

WALK 15
Stepper Point

Start/finish	Padstow Harbour car park: pay and display, toilets (SW 918 754)
Distance	7½ miles/12km
Total ascent	1045ft/320m
Time	4hrs
Terrain	Coastal path along low cliffs and through sand dunes; return through fields
Map	OS Explorer 106 Newquay & Padstow
Nearest town	Padstow

The first part of this walk takes you along the west side of the beautiful Camel Estuary, where huge sandy beaches beckon, then out around the spectacular headland of Stepper Point.

Start by walking along the north side of the harbour, picking up the South West Coast Path towards St Saviour's Point.

Beyond the point you'll enter the head of a lovely little sandy bay, St George's Cove, and as you continue round **Gun Point** you'll reach the wide expanse of sands at **Harbour Cove** (known locally as Tregirls). There's a lovely marram grass dune system here, and as you walk along the low cliffs (unless the tide is out, in which case you'll almost inevitably be down on the beach), you'll get views across the mouth of the estuary over the Doom Bar – a sandbank – to Polzeath.

At Gun Point you'll find the remains of the fortifications that protected Padstow from invaders.

Porthmis
Bri

Trevone
Bay

Newtrain
Bay

Tre

Just off the path is a cast-iron water tank dated 1888, and a granite marker dated 1868, but it was already called **Gun Point** on maps produced in 1801, and the fortifications are thought to date back to the time of the Spanish Armada.

Northwards Stepper Point is calling, and the coast path continues around tiny **Hawker's Cove** and above the little channel of The Narrows to the old lookout station above **Stepper Point**.

The daymark on Stepper Point is known locally as the **Pepperpot**. It was built in 1832 to act as a navigation marker for boats coming into the Camel Estuary.

As you carry on along the coast path there are some interesting geological formations to look out for, such as the

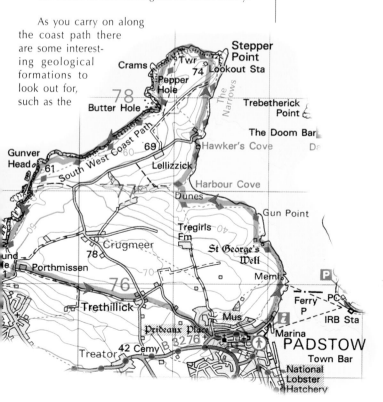

Stepper Point from Pentire Point

Pepper Hole, **Butter Hole** and, further along, the Fox Hole just off **Gunver Head**. These coastal features originated as sea caves; the roofs have fallen in to leave what is known as a blowhole.

Carry on along the clifftop, enjoying the views of the little islands just offshore, then the rocky bays of Longcarrow Cove as you approach Roundhole Point. Here there is another very fine blowhole, known, unsurprisingly, as the **Round Hole**: keep away from the edge.

Immediately beyond Roundhole Point you'll start to cut back inland above lovely **Trevone Bay**. As you curve around the northeast corner of the bay, don't drop down to the beach and the village (unless you have time for a bit of exploration), but take a public footpath on the left, climbing steeply to the farm at **Porthmissen**. As you approach the farm turn right in front of the buildings and follow an old byway across fields to Trethillick Farm.

You reach **Trethillick** at a lane junction. Cross the lane and pick up a continuation public footpath that cuts a corner to bring you out onto the lane again. Turn right and walk into **Padstow**, descending past the church and back to the harbour.

PADSTOW

Padstow is named after the Welsh missionary St Petroc (the original name of the town being Petroc-stow). He landed at nearby Trebetherick around AD500, and after his death a monastery was established here. When the Vikings came to the area in 981 the monks moved inland to Bodmin. In more recent times the town prospered as a fishing port, although today Padstow is best known as a tourist venue, thanks in part to the celebrity chef Rick Stein. The Camel Trail brings visitors in by bicycle; this popular 29km multi-use route follows the old railway line inland to Bodmin and on to Wenfordbridge.

WALK 16

Trevose Head

Start/finish	Constantine Bay, car park overlooking the beach: toilets (SW 858 745)
Distance	5¾ miles/9.25km
Total ascent	650ft/200m
Time	3hrs
Terrain	Sandy beaches and high cliffs; return via heathland and golf course
Map	OS Explorer 106 Newquay & Padstow
Nearest town	Padstow

A lovely walk around this popular headland linking some of the finest beaches in Cornwall. The walk is never taxing, but it is worth taking your time to enjoy the views.

Start by walking down to the beach. Turn north and walk along **Constantine Bay** until some steps lead up over a ridge at the back of the beach. The path leads over to the cliffs above **Booby's Bay** where you can see the remains of a shipwreck.

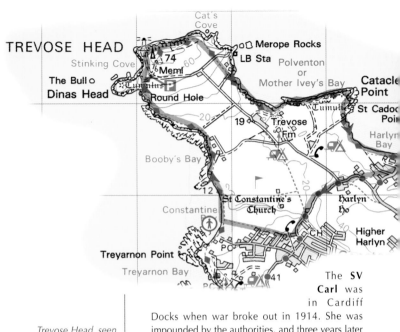

TREVOSE HEAD

Cat's Cove

△ 74
Meml

Stinking Cove

The Bull o
Dinas Head

Round Hole

Merope Rocks

LB Sta

Polventon
or
Mother Ivey's Bay

Catacle
Point

St Cadoc
Poir

19 ○

Trevose
Fm

Booby's Bay

12

Constantine

St Constantine's
Church

Harlyn
Bay

Harlyn
Ho

Higher
Harlyn

Treyarnon Point

Treyarnon Bay

41

*Trevose Head, seen
from Pentire Point*

The **SV Carl** was in Cardiff Docks when war broke out in 1914. She was impounded by the authorities, and three years later it was decided to tow her to London to be broken

up for scrap. During the operation a storm hit the west coast, and the SV *Carl* broke free. Most of the 60ft wreck lay buried under the sand until the huge storms of 2014 revealed her and showed just how well she has been preserved.

Keep left along the clifftop path, going through a kissing gate and continuing to the **Round Hole** just before **Trevose Head**. There are many shipwrecks off the head.

Trevose Head is designated a Site of Special Scientific Interest for its geological and biological attributes. The cliffs are home to breeding fulmars, and there are colonies of nesting razorbills and guillemots. Look out for wild asparagus growing on the cliffs, and shore dock which is found at their base.

From the lighthouse head east along the cliffs, then round the next headland above Chairs Rock and Merope Rocks. Just beyond you'll come to the Trevose Head Lifeboat Station, down on the shore. The path nears the clifftop again as you walk above the narrow inlet of Long Cove, then the broad expanse of **Mother Ivey's Bay**. Continue eastwards to **Cataclews Point** and then the superb **Harlyn Bay**, a popular surfing venue. The coast path runs along the back of the beach and brings you to **Harlyn Bridge**.

At Harlyn Bridge turn right along the lane to find a little lane on the right leading into a small housing estate. Follow this to a public footpath on the left after 100m. Follow the footpath across a couple of fields to emerge on a lane. Turn right and follow the lane around a corner to the left. Continue to a sharp bend right, by a little pond, and here you'll see another lane going straight ahead. Follow this lane across a golf course; as you pass the clubhouse go round a bend to the left, then take a public footpath on the right back to the beach at Constantine Bay.

WALK 17
Kelsey Head and Cubert Common

Start/finish	National Trust car park at Holywell; toilets, café (SW 766 587)
Distance	4¼ miles/6.75km
Total ascent	670ft/205m
Time	2–3hrs
Terrain	Sandy beaches and high cliffs; return via golf course
Map	OS Explorer 104 Redruth & St Agnes
Nearest town	Newquay

Low cliffs around a headland with a dramatic sandy beach on either side; another narrow beach splits the peninsula from the meat of this walk. Allow time to relax on the beaches, and to enjoy the heathland on the linking route over Cubert Common.

Walk from the car park to the public toilets in **Holywell** and head left out onto the beach. This is a lovely stretch of sand, and you should pick up the South West Coast Path which crosses the back of the beach, heading north.

The shipwreck that can be seen at low tide is thought to be the **SS Francia** which was lost in 1917 as it sailed out of Newquay with a cargo of coal. There is some confusion over this, however: some reports state that the *Francia*, a 700-ton steamer from Argentina, was sunk four miles off shore.

The public bridleway at the head of the beach could be taken as a short cut, rejoining the main route on Cubert Common.

Follow the coast path through the dunes and up onto the clifftop, then onto the peninsula known as **Kelsey Head**.

The route is obvious here: keep following the line of cliffs, enjoying the magnificent views as you go. Round the headland you'll find a delightful cove – **Porth Joke** – where seals can often be seen. ◄ The route continues around the head of Porth Joke, and regains the clifftop on **Pentire Point West**, where superb views open out across Crantock Beach to the east.

Follow the coast path all the way around the Point, ignoring the first public footpath to the right. Once you are above **Crantock Beach** look for the second public footpath on the right, which leads southwestwards into the village of **West Pentire**. Turn right along the lane, round a bend to the left, then to the right, and here you'll see a public footpath which leads around a number of fields to a footbridge over a tiny stream at Treago Mill.

Cross the footbridge and you'll join a byway. Turn left, eastwards, along the byway, following the south bank of the stream to reach a junction of tracks below **Treago Farm**. The junction can be a little confusing. Ignore the track to the left (which crosses the stream and goes up to the farm); ignore the little path which goes straight ahead, contouring across the northeastern slopes of Cubert Common. To the right are two more tracks, one climbing steeply up the hill, the second going sharp right, crossing the hill diagonally. Take this last path (a public footpath), which climbs southwestwards to cross the western shoulder of **Cubert Common**.

In 400m go straight over a byway and continue walking to reach another path junction by a spring. Continue straight ahead here over **The Kelseys** past the Holywell Bay Golf Club, and you'll find yourself strolling down the top edge of the dunes into the village of **Holywell**.

WALK 18
St Agnes Head and Beacon

Start/finish	Car park on Trelawny Road in the centre of St Agnes (SW 719 504)
Distance	4½ miles/7.25km
Total ascent	1005ft/305m
Time	3hrs
Terrain	Old lanes, a moorland hill, clifftop paths
Map	OS Explorer 104 Redruth & St Agnes
Nearest town	Redruth

This is a great walk for those wanting to explore a beautiful section of the coast whilst also climbing a prominent little hill. The views from the top of St Agnes Beacon are among the best on the north coast of Cornwall.

Start by walking to the top end of the car park. You'll see a track between the library and the scout hut; follow this out onto Polbreen Lane and turn right to reach a junction. Go straight over into Whitworth Close. In 100m you'll meet another lane coming in from the right, but keep straight on to reach bungalow No 7.

You'll see a signpost for St Agnes Beacon directly opposite the bungalow. Take this path, then turn left onto a narrow lane. Follow this out onto a road, and cross over to reach Beacon Farm. Continue on the green lane, over a stile and across a field with a hedge to your right. Climb a second stile to enter the Open Access land of **St Agnes Beacon**. Turn right here and follow the path directly uphill through heather to the summit.

The two rocks on the summit are known as 'Garder Wartha', and 'Garder Wollas' – 'Upper Seat' and 'Lower Seat'. The nearby mound is the remains of a Bronze Age burial chamber, or barrow, dating from 2000 to 1500BC. There are two other barrows close by.

At the end of the 18th century a tower was built on the summit, and was known variously as St Ann's Summer House, the Pleasure House, or Unwin and Donnithorne's Castle. By the 1850s it was noted that only ruins remained, and it seems likely that the rubble became the base for the OS trig pillar.

Once you've taken in the extensive views eastwards over St Agnes, and along the coast to St Agnes Head to the northwest, head downhill from the Beacon, following a vague path to the northwest to the lane marked on the OS map as Beacon Drive. Cross straight over on a lane that leads towards the coast. Go gently downhill, then pick up a public footpath on the left after 100m that leads through the old mines and out to the South West Coast Path above **Carn Gowla**. ▶ Turn right; ignore the road through the car park, and instead take the coast path that follows the cliffs out to **St Agnes Head**.

The views north to St Agnes Head are matched by the equally wonderful views southwards to Tubby's Head, the cliffs covered with the remains of old engine houses and mining ruins.

The summit of St Agnes Beacon

During the Second World War the land here was part of a Light Anti-Aircraft Practice Camp. The whole area was covered in bungalows and Nissen huts, and even had a theatre. It was later used as a staging post for American army units on their way to France.

Carry on around the Head towards **Newdowns Head** just a short way along the coast. Stay on the clifftop path for the best views down into Polberro Cove, and then descend steps alongside an old mine as the path drops into **Trevaunance Cove**. Enjoy exploring St Agnes before making your way back to the car park. Follow Quay Road south, then at the junction by the Tap House go along British Road to its end. Turn left onto Vicarage Road, then right into Trelawny Road.

WALK 19

Godrevy Point, Navax Point and Hudder Down

Start/finish	Car park at North Cliffs, just off the B3301 (SW 625 431)
Distance	8¼ miles/13.25km
Total ascent	1600ft/490m
Time	5hrs
Terrain	Woodland and river valley path, often boggy; return via high cliffs
Map	OS Explorer 102 Land's End and 104 Redruth & St Agnes
Nearest town	Camborne

This is a superb walk along the lovely Red River valley, out to the huge beach at Gwithian, then a long and beautiful return along the coast via Godrevy Point.

Start by walking back out to B3301 from the car park to a public footpath on the other side of the road. This takes you south along a field margin to Downs Farm where you come to another road. Turn left, then round a bend to the right to another road junction. Turn right here and walk for 100m to where a public bridleway heads off to the southwest alongside the Red River.

> The **Red River** gets its name from the mining wastes that made it a rusty red in colour. Today it is a haven for wildlife, with some particularly special plants and insects, as well as badgers, foxes and otters. Rarities include the scarce blue-tailed damselfly, which was one of the species that saw the establishment of the Red River Rescuers, a local biodiversity action group who manage the reserve.

Follow the delightful wooded path alongside the river for just over a kilometre to reach a path junction. Ignore the path going up to Ashill to the right, and continue along

*Godrevy lighthouse
from below Godrevy
Farm*

the riverside path to **Menadarva** and a minor road. Turn left along the road, then right within 100m, back onto a public footpath again. This passes through the medieval

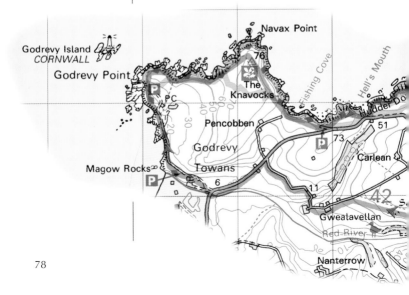

hamlet of Menadarva, then runs uphill to the corner of a field.

There are two public footpaths continuing from here. Take the one to the left, going northwest out to the road near **Gwealavellan**. Turn left along the lane and follow it to a junction with the B3301. Turn left along the B road, and follow it downhill for 500m to Gwithian Bridge. Just before the bridge there is a track on the right which leads into a car park. Pass through the car park and out onto the clifftop path, soon picking up the South West Coast Path. ▸ The track leads on to a further car park (with public toilets). Continue along the path out to **Godrevy Point**.

The views here are spectacular, and the headland of Godrevy with its island just offshore will draw you on.

Beyond Godrevy Island there is a dangerous reef known as **The Stones** extending out into St Ives Bay. Following the loss of the screw steamer *Nile* with all its crew in 1859, public pressure led to Trinity House constructing the lighthouse on the island. It was maintained by a two-man crew until it was automated in 1939. Further modernisation was undertaken in 1995, when it was converted to

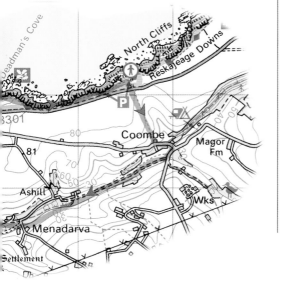

Navax Point from the South West Coast Path above Mutton Cove

Climb up to the OS trig pillar for the best views.

operate with solar power and it is now monitored and controlled from the Trinity House Operations Control Centre at Harwich in Essex.

Continue around the headland, looking for seals down in Mutton Cove and Kynance Cove as you go. The next headland is **Navax Point**. ◀ Here there are two paths, one uphill to the trig pillar, the other hugging the cliffs.

The route now is very straightforward, passing above Castle Giver Cove and **Fishing Cove** as you come back close to the B3301. The South West Coast Path clings to the clifftops above Hell's Mouth at **Hudder Down** and on to Hudder Cove, then finally along the long stretch over **North Cliffs** and back to your car.

PENWITH AND
WEST CORNWALL

Walkers setting out at Cape Cornwall (Walk 27)

WALK 20

The Hayle Estuary Nature Reserves

Start/finish	Public pay and display car park on Commercial Road overlooking Copperhouse Pool on the B3301 in Hayle: toilets (SW 563 378)
Distance	5 miles/8km
Total ascent	215ft/65m
Time	2hrs
Terrain	Level pavements and roads; some muddy sections on nature reserve paths
Map	OS Explorer 102 Land's End
Nearest town	Hayle

This is a different kind of walk, taking you through the town of Hayle but connecting three superb RSPB Nature Reserves. You can do the route in its entirety, or just visit the reserves individually if time is pressing.

The Hayle Estuary is owned by the RSPB – The Royal Society for the Protection of Birds.

Start the walk by following the very obvious and easy path anti-clockwise around the edge of **Copperhouse Pool**; the route is very clear, and follows the pavement of the B3301 for a short distance.

> **Copperhouse Pool** is a great place to look for waders and wildfowl. Shelducks breed here and can often be seen feeding with their young in the summer; it's also possible to get close views of lapwings, oystercatchers and curlew, and occasionally little egrets. In the summer you'll see common terns fishing in the shallow water.

At the eastern end of the Pool cross a footbridge, then head up to and then along the north side. Continue all the way round the western end where the Pool empties into the Hayle Estuary, and cross a bridge here to regain the B3301. Turn right along the road and follow it south, under the railway line, then round to the right to go back under the railway again. Keep to the left side of the road until you reach a pelican crossing, and cross here to find a public footpath which takes you to **Carnsew Pool**, the second reserve on this walk. Once again walk anticlockwise, keeping an eye out for birds on the water as you go.

Carnsew Pool is probably the best place to get really close to wildlife on this walk. In winter you might be lucky enough to see black-throated, red-throated and great northern divers. In late summer the muddy western end of Carnsew Pool is a regular stopping off point for waders starting their migration. Look for oystercatchers, curlew, black-tailed and bar-tailed godwits, turnstone, grey plover, golden plover, ringed plover and whimbrel.

The raised walkway around Carnsew Pool gives great views across the Hayle Estuary,

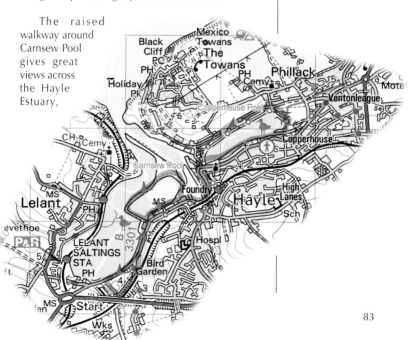

Look for greenshanks on the Hayle Nature Reserves

and eventually re-emerges onto the B3301 at the southwest corner. Turn right and follow the road (The Causeway) alongside Lelant Saltings to the entrance to the small Ryan's Field RSPB Reserve on the opposite side of the road. Cross the road and follow the waymarked trail anticlockwise around the small lagoon.

> **Lelant Saltings** is renowned for large congregations of teal and wigeon throughout the winter months. Ryan's Pool is tidal, but is one of the last parts of the estuary to flood, so as the tide comes keep an eye out for all manner of waders and ducks. They are forced off the main part of the estuary by the incoming tide, and find refuge here.

Once you've explored Ryan's Pool head back along the B3301 to **Carnsew Pool**. Turn left down the first public footpath you come across, but turn right along the south side of the Pool, parallel to the B3301. On reaching the path that you took to enter Carnsew Pool, turn right onto the road again and retrace your steps back to the bridge over the western end of **Copperhouse Pool**. Keep along the flat path to the south side of Copperhouse Pool and you'll soon be back at your car.

WALK 21
Wicca Pool and Zennor Head

Start/finish	Zennor village: car park by the Old Chapel Backpackers & Café; honesty box (SW 453 384)
Distance	5¼ miles/8.5km
Total ascent	950ft/290m
Time	3hrs
Terrain	Ancient field system and high clifftop paths
Map	OS Explorer 102 Land's End
Nearest town	St Ives

This is a really great coastal walk enjoying some truly spectacular scenery. The first part of the route is through a myriad of fields – a glance at the 1:25,000 map will show hundreds of tiny fields, a sure sign of the antiquity of this age-old farming system in the South West peninsula.

From the car park turn left along the lane to reach the church, then follow the public footpath that starts to the left of the churchyard. The path splits almost immediately, with the footpath (right) going off through fields, and a public bridleway heading northwest. Stay on the public footpath and follow it through the maze of fields, heading for the lane at **Tremedda Farm** away to the northeast.

Once you reach the lane cross straight over, and continue along the footpath to **Lower Tregerthen**. Here you keep to the right of the farm, and again go straight ahead when you reach the farm access track. The route now goes downhill through yet more tiny fields to cross the head of a stream – the same stream that you'll cross again later in the walk as you traverse Wicca Cliff.

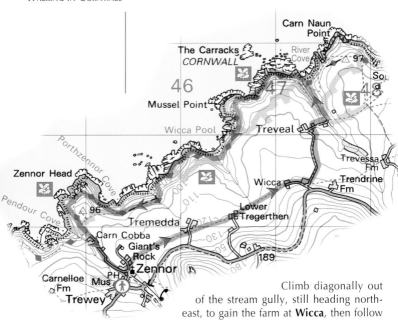

Climb diagonally out of the stream gully, still heading northeast, to gain the farm at **Wicca**, then follow the more obvious track eastwards to Boscubben Farm.

Walk to the right of the farm at Boscubben, but don't walk out onto the B3306. About 100m before the main road a public footpath goes off to the left. Follow this for 50m, then turn left again, heading in a general northerly direction gently downhill towards the farm at **Treveal** (SW 473 400). As you approach the farm at Treveal, take a sharp right and descend very steeply along the footpath to Trevail Mill at the bottom of a steep-sided gorge. At the Mill turn left and walk along the stream's west side down to the footbridge overlooking the lovely **River Cove**. ◀

Turn westwards along the footpath that cuts across the slope. The route – now along the South West Coast Path – is very obvious, and you soon round a headland to reach Treveal Cliff above Economy Cove.

There is a path leading down into River Cove, a great spot for a picnic. However, you do have to climb back up again to continue the walk.

Off shore lie **The Carracks**, a small group of islands, while in the cove below you may be lucky enough to see grey seals hauled out on the rocks.

Continue around **Mussel Point**, then across Wicca Cliff with the deep channels of Cornelias Zawn and Wicca Pool down to your right. The way descends beyond Wicca Cliff to cross the stream that you encountered earlier near Lower Tregerthen, then ascends the other side to reach the headland of Tregerthen Cliff above Carn Porth.

The path beyond Tregerthen Cliff cuts down almost to the waterline across some steep ground; look out for the flat slabs of Gala Rocks just below you. The path encounters another deep gully before climbing very steeply up the east side of the stream. Cross over the stream high up in the gully and follow the route westwards across Tremedda Cliff.

Cross an old wall that runs down towards the sea far below, and 100m beyond this reach a path junction. Take the one to the right (the official Coast Path), descending slightly above **Porthzennor Cove**, then up to the top of

Zennor village

Zennor Cliff high above **Zennor Head**. A little inland lies the OS triangulation pillar at 96m, and a steep climb leads to this superb viewpoint.

To the west of Zennor Head the coast cuts in at the gorgeous **Pendour Cove**. Our route leaves the Coast Path and follows the public footpath south to Zennor village, along the east side of the valley and stream that flows into Pendour Cove. Treat yourself to a refreshing drink at the historic Tinners Arms.

WALK 22
Zennor Hill

Start/finish	Zennor village: car park by the Old Chapel Backpackers & Café; honesty box (SW 453 384)
Distance	1¾ miles/2.75km
Total ascent	415ft/125m
Time	1hr
Terrain	Moorland paths and tracks, peaty in places
Map	OS Explorer 102 Land's End
Nearest town	St Ives

There is something magical about Zennor Hill. It's certainly not a big hill, but it commands fine views of the coast, and gives an opportunity for a short hill walk for those based in this lovely part of Cornwall.

From the car park turn right along the lane and out onto the B3306. Turn right along the road for about 50m, and look for a public footpath on the left that heads southeast up the valley. Keep on the obvious path that follows the east side of the stream. Walk for 800m until just beyond the turn for the old farm at **Rosemorran** up on the left. Here you'll see a permissive footpath climbing up the hill to your left. Follow this through the intricate ancient field system and out onto the open hill just below the summit

Zennor Hill from the lane out of Zennor village

of the hill. ▶ Climb the south ridge to the summit of **Zennor Hill** (237m), passing the logan stone on the way. From the summit descend just north of west along a good path. It's quite steep in places but the way is obvious, and it soon takes you down to the B3306 near a telephone exchange. Turn left along the road, then right at the lane that leads back to the church in **Zennor**.

Near the top of Zennor Hill is a fine logan (or rocking) stone.

89

WALK 23
Gurnard's Head

Start/finish	Ask at The Gurnard's Head pub at Treen if you can park there, perhaps popping for a beer or a meal afterwards? (SW 436 375). A couple of cars could be squeezed in by the farm at Higher Porthmeer: do not block buildings or gateways (SW 432 371).
Distance	3 miles/4.75km
Total ascent	980ft/300m
Time	2hrs
Terrain	Field footpaths, sometimes muddy; clifftop path and return via quiet road
Map	OS Explorer 102 Land's End
Nearest town	St Ives

This part of the Cornish coast feels as far removed from the rest of England as it is possible to be. The coastal scenery here is sublime – you could just as easily be walking along a clifftop in Shetland or the Outer Hebrides! However, the inland countryside is uniquely Cornish, and it's a great combination. One of my favourite walks in Cornwall.

Start by walking north from the sharp bend in the B3306 through the hamlet of **Treen**. As the lane leaves the buildings behind and bends to the right two public footpaths lead ahead, one to the left (which you can follow for a slightly shorter version of this walk), and one going to the right, which is the path to take.

It is possible to get down to the lovely beach in Treen Cove, but it's not an easy descent or reascent.

The paths cuts across the field to the right, then runs north through a series of small enclosures and down to the old mines at Lean Point. Turn left here on the South West Coast Path, above **Treen Cove**. ◄

There is evidence of an Iron Age fort on the top of Gurnard's Head, called Trereen Dinas.

Carry on along the main path westwards, passing the ruins of **Chapel Jane**. Across the west side of Treen Cove you can see the long, rocky headland of Gurnard's Head. ◄

The ruined chapel has almost all fallen into the sea. The 'Jane' has nothing to do with the girl's name, but comes from the Cornish *yein*, which means 'bleak'. The name **Gurnard's Head** comes from the fact that the headland is said to be the same shape as the fish.

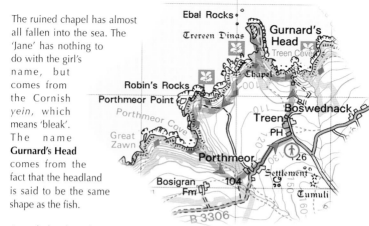

A path leads right out onto **Gurnard's Head**, and it is well worth doing this unless it is very windy, or you are not too good with heights. The way is obvious, but the ridge

Gurnard's Head from the path above Treen Cove

connecting the head to the mainland is quite narrow, and the rocks underfoot can be slippery when wet.

Return along the narrow ridge to the 'mainland'. Climb steeply uphill, then turn right along the South West Coast Path, heading west. The route is easy to follow. Continue around the next headland, **Porthmeor Point**, and round into the delightful **Porthmeor Cove**. The path descends diagonally down to the south, and you can go out onto the sandy beach in the cove to explore.

When you're ready to return to the Gurnard's Head pub, follow the Coast Path a short way up the west side of the little valley that leads into Porthmeor Cove. Here you'll come to a public footpath heading up the south side of the valley, in a southeasterly direction. Climb steeply up the gorge to another junction of paths. Here go left, down to the stream. Cross over via a footbridge and climb up the other side to the farm at Lower Porthmeor. Cross a track and continue in the same direction out to the B3306. Turn left along the road and walk the short distance back to the Gurnard's Head, in time for a drink.

WALK 24

*Hannibal's Carn, the Nine Maidens
and Mên-an-Tol*

Start/finish	From the B3306 turn southeast at Trevowhan towards Lanyon Quoit, and park on the roadside on Bosullow Common (SW 418 344)
Distance	4¼ miles/6.75km
Total ascent	500ft/155m
Time	3hrs
Terrain	Moorland, boggy in places, at times pathless; return via quiet lane; navigation skills essential
Map	OS Explorer 102 Land's End
Nearest town	St Just

This is a slightly contrived route linking together three important archaeological sites that are scattered around White Downs. However, the route is a great way of visiting these sites at the same time as having a very enjoyable walk.

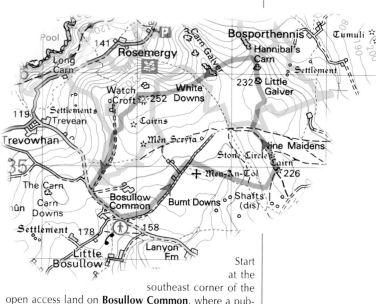

Start at the southeast corner of the open access land on **Bosullow Common**, where a public footpath crosses the road. Walk along the clear track to the northeast, following the old lane out onto open access land at **Burnt Downs** (SW 424 348). Continue until you come to the open moor and a small path on the right leads through the moorland grasses and heather to **Mên-an-Tol**.

Mên-an-Tol, also known locally as the Crick Stone, is a group of three stones. One is a round stone on end, with a large hole in its middle, while the other two are standing stones. There are other

Mên an Tol

standing stones and burial mounds nearby. Mên-an-Tol is believed to date from the late Neolithic period. Some think the stones are the remains of a stone circle, in which case they have been rearranged, while others suggest that the stone with the hole may have been a capstone for one of the nearby burial chambers.

The first excavation of the site was by William Borlase in 1749. Fortunately Borlase drew a plan, showing that the stones were not in the same position as they are today. Borlase also stated that local farmers had removed some of the stones for use elsewhere.

Continue along the faint path beyond Mên-an-Tol, aiming towards the distant Ding Dong Mine. The path veers slightly to the east, and you should follow it until you reach an old boundary wall. Turn north along this and climb a short rise to a hill with an ancient cairn (SW 434 349). A path heads off just west of north and takes you in 200m to the **Nine Maidens** of Boskednan.

The **Nine Maidens** are actually the 10 standing stones that remain of an original 22. The granite blocks stand about 1m high, although only six stand upright, and one more protrudes about half a metre out of the soil. William Borlase also excavated here, in 1754, and he found 19 stones. It is thought that the Nine Maidens date from the Bronze Age.

Continue just north of northwest along the high ground, passing another standing stone and a burial mound, then leave the path where it swings off towards the northwest and make for the corner of the old field system just west of the little hill at 233m (SW 434 356). Pass through a small rectangular field onto the top of the hill, then turn left and follow the delightful, narrowing ridge over **Little Galver** to **Hannibal's Carn**.

Don't continue walking down the ridge to the north, but instead follow the ancient boundary line westwards towards the upper hill of **Carn Galver**, to spot height 249m (SW 427 360). Walk southwest and cross a public footpath. Climb over the next boundary and continue westwards towards the OS triangulation pillar on **Watch Croft** at 252m (SW 420 357). There are yet more cairns and standing stones here on what was once an important look-out post.

Head southwest over rough ground to gain a good track along which a public bridleway runs. Turn south (left), thankfully after all that pathless terrain, and follow the track out to the lane on Bosullow Common. Turn left to get back to your car.

WALK 25
Chûn Quoit and Castle

Start/finish	Car park on Woon Gumpus Common, off the B3318 south of Pendeen (SW 393 333)
Distance	2½ miles/4km
Total ascent	190ft/60m
Time	1.5hrs
Terrain	Good moorland paths
Map	OS Explorer 102 Land's End
Nearest town	St Just

This is a short walk to one of the most important Iron Age hill forts in Cornwall. It's a great walk in itself, but can be combined with other routes nearby to give a longer day if you want.

From the car park you'll see two tracks heading roughly east. One goes northeast (left: the return route), while the second, more easterly (but less obvious) track is the one to take. The route goes roughly eastwards over the moor, and you pick up a better track at an ancient field enclosure after 700m. It is now much clearer, and takes you

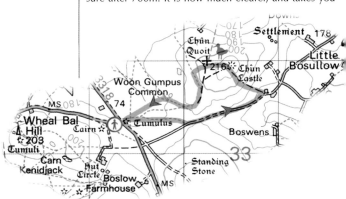

around the south side of the obvious hill of Chûn Downs off to your left.

Walk to the road head at Trehyllys Farm (SW 408 336), then turn left and walk steeply uphill to the north-west, to gain the top of Chûn Downs and the remarkable **Chûn Castle**.

> **Chûn Castle** is a 2500-year-old hill fort. It takes its name from the Cornish words *chi* and *woon*, which together mean 'House on the Downs'. It is thought that it was built to protect the nearby tin and copper mines.

To the west, about 500m away, is **Chûn Quoit**. Once you've finished exploring the Castle, head over to the Quoit.

> A quoit is all that remains of a megalithic tomb dating from the Neolithic period. There are many quoits still in existence in Cornwall, although 'dolmen' is another terms used to name them.

Walk south along a path over Higher Downs, then pick up the main track that skirts an old boundary wall to a little pond, before taking you back over **Woon Gumpus Common** to your car.

Chûn Quoit, one of the best examples of a dolmen in the Southwest peninsula

WALK 26

Pendeen Watch and the Levant Mines

Start/finish	Park on the main road in Trewellard, near the junction of the B3306 and B3318 (SW 376 338)
Distance	4 miles/6.5km
Total ascent	740ft/225m
Time	2.5hrs
Terrain	Field paths and quiet country lanes; section along high cliffs
Map	OS Explorer 102 Land's End
Nearest town	St Just

This walk leads you through some of the most important historic tin-mining areas in the whole of the UK. There is much to see, not only in the way of industrial archaeology, but also in the spectacular views along this section of coast.

Start by walking northeast along the main road, towards Pendeen. Pass the turning for Geevor Mine and look for a public footpath on the left just a short way further on.

GEEVOR TIN MINE

This mine operated between 1911 and 1990, during which time about 50,000 tons of black tin were produced. Tin had been mined in the area since the 18th century; in the 1880s over 170 workers were employed at the mine, but by 1891 it had closed.

The outbreak of the Boer War in South Africa forced many miners who had emigrated to return to Cornwall, and a group of miners from St Just decided to lease the land where the old mine was situated and to try making a business out of it. They set up the Levant North–Wheal Geevor Company in 1901. In 1904 they sold the enterprise to the West Australian Gold Field Company Ltd, who in 1911 brought together a number of local mining companies to establish the Geevor Tin Mines Ltd.

Geevor Tin Mine is now a museum and heritage centre and is a major attraction in this part of Cornwall.

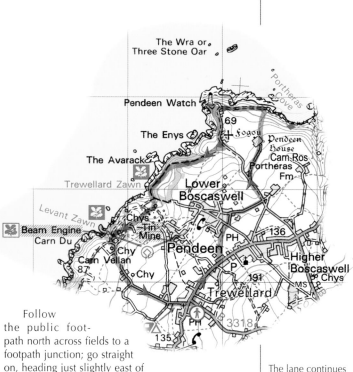

Follow the public footpath north across fields to a footpath junction; go straight on, heading just slightly east of north into **Lower Boscaswell**. On reaching a road turn left, then right immediately down a lane that leads to a little road triangle. From here head east along a lane to a T-junction where you should turn left downhill to Pendeen Gate. ▶

At Pendeen Gate turn right along a byway that goes to **Pendeen House**. Keep to the right of the house and pick up the public footpath that leads downhill to the coast at Pendeen Cliff. ▶

Turn westwards along the South West Coast Path and climb steeply and diagonally up to the lighthouse at **Pendeen Watch**.

The lane continues from here to the lighthouse at Pendeen Watch.

The views from Pendeen Cliff eastwards over the gorgeous beach at Portheras Cove and the little islands of The Kenidjacks are superb.

99

The lighthouse at Pendeen Watch

Pendeen Lighthouse – or Pendeen Watch as it is invariably known – was built in 1891 by Trinity House. It is still in use today, and was automated in 1995. The cottages around the lighthouse are now leased out as holiday lets.

Once you've enjoyed the views from the lighthouse along the coast westwards follow the lane inland for 400m, until you come to a South West Coast Path signpost pointing west along the clifftop. Follow the obvious path above Pendeen Old Cliff and out to **Carn Rôs**.

Ahead is one of the most fascinating stretches of coastline: a vast area of interesting remains of old tin mines at Trewallard Bottoms, Geevor and Levant. Many people spend all day here just exploring.

Levant Mine was established in 1820 to bring tin and copper ore from deep beneath the sea. The mine was over 600m deep, and became known as 'the mine under the sea' as many of the tunnels ran

Levant Mine and one of the old engine houses

under the seabed for up to a mile. The mine used what is now the world's only surviving example of a Cornish beam engine, and this is still operational. There is a small museum on site, which is well worth a visit.

Once you've finished exploring continue along the clifftop path until you're at the old **Levant Mine**, then walk inland to the mine car park. Follow the track southwards, inland, climbing gently into Hillside and the village of **Trewellard**.

WALK 27
The Kenidjack Valley and Cape Cornwall

Start/finish	From St Just head west down Cape Cornwall Road; public toilets and car park at lane end, overlooking Cape Cornwall (SW 353 317)
Distance	4¼ miles/6.75km
Total ascent	895ft/270m
Time	3hrs
Terrain	High cliffs and field paths, muddy in places
Map	OS Explorer 102 Land's End
Nearest town	St Just

The headland of Cape Cornwall is such an obvious target on this walk that it is tempting to go straight out there, but it does make a superb finale to this route which also utilises a stretch of the South West Coast Path.

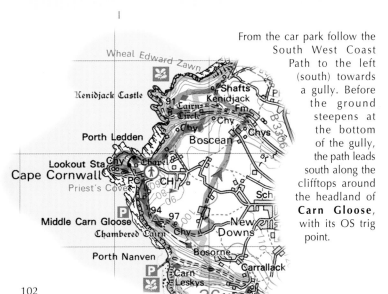

From the car park follow the South West Coast Path to the left (south) towards a gully. Before the ground steepens at the bottom of the gully, the path leads south along the clifftops around the headland of **Carn Gloose**, with its OS trig point.

Here you'll find the impressive **Ballowall Barrow** chambered cairn, and a little further along, the Barrow Cairn.

You hit a tarmac lane at this point and should walk along it, passing a chimney on the left, and continuing to a sharp right bend. Here there is a public footpath on the left that you can follow to Ballowal Farm. Keep the farm buildings to your left and continue along the footpath to reach Cape Cornwall Road. The footpath continues just across the road to the right. Walk along field edges to a footpath junction; go straight ahead here with Boswedden House a way off to your left. The footpath heads northeast to reach the end of another little lane at **Boscean** (SW 363 321). At this point another lane goes straight ahead, down into the head of a valley at **Kenidjack Farm**. Follow this, over a stream, to the road head at the farm. Take the byway on the left, running along the north side of the stream and heading west towards the coast.

After 200m (from the road head at Kenidjack Farm) there is a track junction. Ignore the one continuing down

Kenidjack Castle from St Helen's Chapel

the valley, and take the path up to the right that leads out to the fabulous headland at **Kenidjack Castle**. Once you get to the clifftop, turn west and follow the South West Coast Path along to the ancient cairn circle overlooking the wonderfully named sea inlet called Zawn Buzz & Gen.

Now the path descends diagonally through an amazing array of prehistoric fields into the Kenidjack Valley. ◄

In the valley bottom a path heads out to the bay and it's definitely worth going down that way for a picnic on the shore.

As well as common and grey seals, you might also catch sight of one of the UK's rarest birds – the **chough** – on this section of coastline. This red-legged member of the crow family was once on the verge of extinction in England, but numbers have been increasing since these magnificent birds returned of their own accord in 2001 (see Introduction). The offspring of those first returning birds can now be seen in many parts of Cornwall, and the headland here and around Cape Cornwall is a very good place to look for them.

The tower that marks the summit of Cape Cornwall

104

Even in Wales and Scotland, where choughs are a little more common, they have traditionally been known as the 'crow of Cornwall' since at least the 17th century.

Now climb back up the valley to a major path junction, just 100m short of the obvious chimney near **Boscean**. Turn right here and climb steeply to the clifftop, soon rejoining the Coast Path and turning left, keeping close by the cliffs all the way out to the headland of **Cape Cornwall**, an important headland since at least the Late Bronze Age. Pottery from that time has been found here.

A permissive path takes you up the east ridge of the Cape to the lookout station. Follow the path on the south side of the Cape and you'll soon be back at the car park.

WALK 28

The Cot Valley from St Just

Start/finish	Large car park in St Just, opposite the tourist information centre (SW 369 312)
Distance	3 miles/4.75km
Total ascent	515ft/155m
Time	2hrs
Terrain	Field paths, often muddy; short section of clifftop walking
Map	OS Explorer 102 Land's End
Nearest town	St Just

This is a lovely short walk from St Just down to the beach at Porth Nanven, and returning through the Cot Valley.

Start by heading to the library (where you will also find the TIC). Facing the library, walk to your left along Lafrowda Close, then turn left along Bosorne Terrace. This becomes South Place. Continue along South Place,

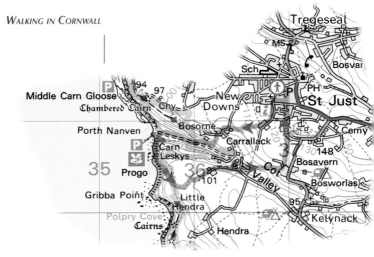

following the lane slightly downhill to the farm at **Carrallack**. Just beyond the farm a public footpath on the right leaves the road and you should follow this west, downhill, to the lane at **Bosorne**.

Turn left on the lane, around a sharp right bend, then a sharp left. Just around the left bend a track heads off to your right; go down this for about 50m until a public footpath on the left leads across a couple of fields and downhill. The path takes a sharp right, then drops diagonally to the bottom of the **Cot Valley** where you again pick up the lane from Bosorne.

Follow the road down to the shore. It's worth spending a bit of time on the beach – **Porth Nanven** – beyond the little car park.

Walk back up the lane beyond the car park to where a Coast Path sign points up the hill to the south (right). It's very steep at first, but the path is easy to follow as it turns around the west side of Hermon Hill, with a steep drop down to the sea. The views to the south are of the headland at Land's End. ◄

On a clear day you can easily see the Isles of Scilly from anywhere along this most westerly coast on Cornwall.

Follow the path around Hermon Hill to reach the clifftop on the south side. Gain the boundary wall at the

Coastal scenery below St Just

top and walk north to the flat area above Carn Gribba. You'll see a public footpath heading inland. Follow this, slightly uphill at first, then along to Letcha before descending to the **Cot Valley** by the youth hostel. The path goes to the south of the hostel, and out along the drive. Turn right at the junction, then in 50m (before the junction with the tarmac public road) turn left along a public footpath that takes you down to cross the stream in the Cot Valley.

Immediately over the stream there is a path junction. Take the path to the right, heading eastwards diagonally up the hill. Cross fields to the farms at **Bosavern**, but don't go out onto the B3306 here. As you approach Bosavern go through the yard to the north side to find a public footpath heading north towards St Just. Off to the right as you walk you'll see the twin radio masts of Higher Bosavern. The path goes to the left of the hill with the radio mast, to emerge on a lane going into **St Just**. Go straight ahead at the crossroads, then take a left at the end to get back to the car park.

THE INLAND MINING DISTRICTS

A mine ruin near Gwennap Pit (Walk 31)

WALK 29
The Porkellis Engine Houses

Start/finish	Poldark Mine Visitor Centre car park (SW 682 314)
Distance	3¾ miles/6km
Total ascent	305ft/95m
Time	2hrs
Terrain	Quiet country lanes, return via a bridleway
Map	OS Explorer 103 The Lizard
Nearest town	Helston

This is a lovely walk that makes a fine Sunday morning stroll, especially if you time it so that you can have lunch at the Star Inn in Porkellis halfway round. The route is mainly on country lanes, and is very easy to follow.

From **Poldark Mine** walk northeast along the lane in the direction of Lower Porthkellis. The lane follows a little stream that flows out from **Porkellis Moor**, and this is a particularly good place to look for wild birds as you walk.

The lane crosses the moor and then brings you to Lower Porkellis. Just beyond there is a junction. Go left here and follow the lane uphill to **Porkellis** where you'll find the delightful Star Inn.

Walk on to the T-junction and turn left along the lane, passing the village chapel. The road takes you downhill to a junction where you should go straight on over Porkellis Bridge. Follow the lane uphill, around a bend to the right at the top, then left at **Darracot**. Just beyond Darracot Farm the lane dips into a little gully and here, just over a stream, you'll see a public bridleway going off to the left. Follow this track, southwards, to Higher Trenear Farm. As you approach the farm the bridleway goes right (onto the B3297), but to the right of the farm

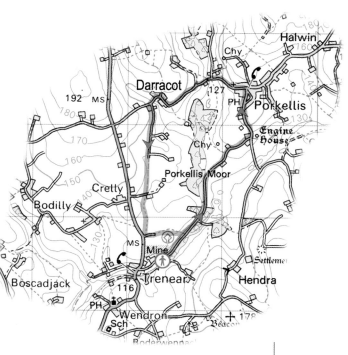

building you'll see a public footpath going dead ahead. Take this footpath along field margins to a path junction in a little layby on the B3297 (SW 681 317).

Turn left along the public footpath, walking eastwards gently downhill to emerge on the lane just along from the **Poldark Mine**. Turn right and retrace your steps back to the car park, hopefully in time for a tour of the mine.

> **Poldark Mine** is within the Wendron Mining District and is one of the oldest in Cornwall; there is evidence of tin mining here in prehistoric times. It is now a very good tourist attraction having been rescued in 2000 from the hands of the receivers.

*The Poldark Mine
Visitor Centre*

It was originally worked in its present state from between 1720 and 1780, and was then known as Wheal Roots Mine.

WALK 30
Carn Brea and Piece

Start/finish	Park in the hamlet of Piece, being careful not to block access to houses or fields – if you ask nicely at The Countryman Inn they may let you use their large car park (SW 678 397)
Distance	2¾ miles/4.5km
Total ascent	360ft/110m
Time	2hrs
Terrain	Field and moorland paths, boggy in places
Map	OS Explorer 104 Redruth & St Agnes
Nearest town	Camborne

An interesting hill walk giving great views over the towns of Camborne and Redruth, and well worth taking your time over. Why not plan an evening walk to the top of Carn Brea, a good place for watching the sun go down?

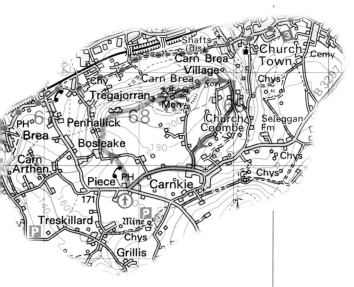

Start this great little hill walk by following the public footpath from the east side of the Countryman Inn. Keep to the left of the obvious mine shaft and emerge from the field into a track. Turn left here, then right through a gate on a footpath where there are often bales of hay stored by a clump of trees. Cut across the field diagonally to the northwest and you'll reach the lane known as Chapel Hill on the north side of a farm (**Bosleake**). Turn right here and walk for a short distance to find an obvious track on your right.

Take this track heading first east, then north into the open access land of Carn Brea.

CARN BREA

The granite hill of Carn Brea dominates this entire area. Its associated mineral resources brought great wealth to the district, the mineral lodes being exploited by some of the richest, and deepest, 18th-century copper and 19th-century tin mines in the world. As you stand atop Carn Brea it doesn't take much imagination to realise that the area was the most important and complex of the mining districts now within the Cornwall and West Devon Mining Landscape World Heritage Site (established in 2006). It was home to many of the key figures in the development of mining and allied technologies and witnessed the widespread urbanisation of what had historically been a rural landscape.

The views northwards here are over the towns of Camborne and Redruth towards the coast. ◄

The track is obvious throughout as you gain the western end of the Carn Brea ridge by a lovely little granite tor. ◄ High up on the ridge you come to a junction of paths. Go straight ahead, making for the summit of **Carn Brea**.

CARN BREA CASTLE

Rising from the summit of Carn Brea, this 14th-century granite building was extensively rebuilt by the Basset family in the 18th century. It is thought to have been originally used as a chapel, before becoming a hunting lodge. Today it is privately owned and run as a restaurant. On the highest point of the ridge stands the Basset Memorial, a 90ft (27m) Celtic cross, built in 1836 in memory of Francis Basset, 1st Baron de Dunstanville and Basset.

This is a tunnel connecting the summit of Carn Brea with the town of Redruth below, but it is probably an old mine shaft, rather than a cave used by smugglers. The town council blocked it off in the 1980s to keep children out. Another tunnel between the summit and St Euny's Church was blocked in 1970.

From the summit continue to head east downhill to reach the bridleway that skirts the eastern flank of the hill. Here you'll meet a number of other paths and tracks. Turn south here (right). After 250m, where the bridleway turns sharply to the left, go southwestwards along a track that brings you out at a lane running south from the summit of Carn Brea. Turn left and walk along the lane to a T-junction. Turn right along the road and follow this back to **Piece**.

WALK 31
Redruth and Gwennap Pit

Start/finish	Redruth, New Cut car park pay and display, toilets (SW 698 421)
Distance	3 miles/4.75km
Total ascent	240ft/70m
Time	2hrs
Terrain	Level pavements through town; footpath to Gwennap Pit
Map	OS Explorer 104 Redruth & St Agnes
Nearest town	Redruth

This is a linear walk to the impressive site of Gwennap Pit. The route can be followed one way or the other, using a taxi to get there or back, or you can simply walk it in both directions. The distance and time above is calculated for a there-and-back walk.

Start by walking to the right down New Cut from the car park entrance. Take a right at the T-junction onto Green Lane, and follow this down to Fore Street. Turn right then left onto Alma Place. At the end of Alma Place turn right onto Bond Street and go under the railway. You'll pass Basset Street on the left, then come to Heanton Terrace by the church. Turn along here, and walk until you reach the junction with Sea View Terrace (left) and Albany Road

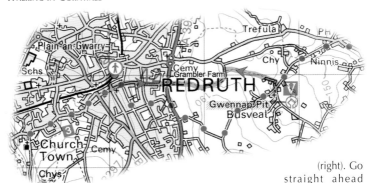

(right). Go straight ahead into Raymond Road. Ignore all turnings to left and right until you reach the A393, known as Sandy Lane, at the northeast corner of a field to your right.

Slight left, across Sandy Lane, is a narrow lane that goes to **Grambler Farm**. Follow this, keeping the farm buildings to your left. The track, which is a public

Gwennap Pit provides a perfect open-air stage

bridleway throughout, continues to a T-junction. Keep left here, and walk north for 100m to another track to your right. This is a public footpath that takes you initially through a scrubby area, then along the north side of a little field. Go through a gap in the hedge in the east

The entrance to the Methodist Chapel at Gwennap Pit

GWENNAP PIT

This wonderful open-air amphitheatre is thought to have been created due to mining subsidence in the mid-18th century, but was found to have remarkable acoustics. As such it became a favoured venue for the Methodist preacher John Wesley. He described it as both a 'round green hollow', and as 'an amphitheatre', and preached there 18 times between 1762 and 1789. After Wesley's death the local people turned the pit into a more regular shape and built the turf seats that we see today. It is used on sunny Sundays for worship still, as well as for musical events, drama and occasional weddings.

Gwennap Pit is included in the Cornwall and West Devon Mining Landscape World Heritage Site (usually known as 'Cornish Mining': see Walk 30). This puts it right up there with the likes of the Taj Mahal, the Great Wall of China, Stonehenge and St Kilda!

corner and follow the obvious path eastwards across the next field, through a hedge and out to a farm on the edge of the village of **Busveal**. Follow the path, now more of a distinct track, eastwards, then around a bend to the right, then left again to reach a junction. Turn right along the lane, then left immediately to reach the chapel at **Gwennap Pit**.

The walk ends here at Gwennap Pit, so once you've enjoyed the peace and tranquillity of the amphitheatre, and perhaps visited the chapel and little museum, simply retrace your steps back to **Redruth Station**.

LAND'S END

The view towards Lamorna Cove from the coast path to Mousehole

WALK 32
Carn Brea, Carn Euny and Bartinney Downs

Start/finish	Follow the road west from the village of Sancreed; park sensibly where a byway heads southwest in a wooded area (SW 403 297)
Distance	4½ miles/7.25km
Total ascent	555ft/170m
Time	2–3hrs
Terrain	Byways and bridleways; moorland, often boggy
Map	OS Explorer 102 Land's End
Nearest town	Penzance

A fascinating moorland walk around a wealth of important archaeological sites, and a great route for those with an interest in wildlife. The views from the top of Carn Brea are stunning.

There is a track running southwest from the road. This byway passes through a narrow strip of woodland to the farm at Higher Trevarthen. Keep going along the track, with the farm to your left. After 500m you'll come to a junction of paths and tracks beside a small marshy area on the left with a little pool.

Continue along the track, bending to the right and passing a farm, then to the left to a junction by another farm. Bear left here and follow the track to the impressive **Carn Euny** ancient village site.

Carn Euny is one of the best-preserved ancient villages in the South West peninsula. There is evidence of occupation from about the 5th century BC through until the late Roman era. You can see the foundations of many houses, giving you a clear idea of the whole village layout, and there is also an intriguing underground passage, known as a 'fogou'.

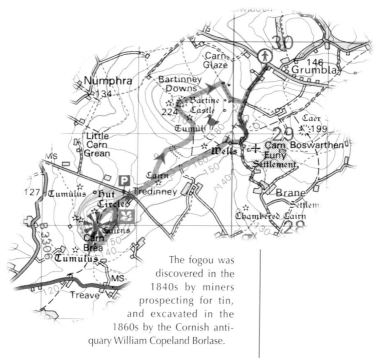

The fogou was discovered in the 1840s by miners prospecting for tin, and excavated in the 1860s by the Cornish antiquary William Copeland Borlase.

Once you've finished exploring Carn Euny head back out along the access track as far as the junction by the farm and turn right again, but only for about 50m. Look for a track to the left that takes you west to St Euny's Chapel and a pair of ancient **wells**.

William Borlase (not the same one who excavated at Carn Euny!) came here in the 1750s, and wrote about meeting two women who told him that 'people who had a mind to receive any benefit from St Euny's Well must come and wash upon the three first Wednesdays in May'.

Just west of the wells you enter open access land. Follow the path southwest over moorland, along the south side of the access land, passing through the china

*Look out for adders
basking on Bartinney
Downs*
clay works of **Tredinney Common**. Continue southwest,
aiming for the obvious dome of Carn Brea.

You'll come to a minor road. Cross over, aiming
slightly right to the car park, and climb up the clear track
that leads to the summit of **Carn Brea** at 198m (SW 385
280). The summit granite outcrops are quite small com-
pared to other Cornish tors, but the views are superb,
taking in the west coast towards Land's End and Cape
Cornwall.

CARN BREA

Not to be confused with the hill of the same name above Redruth and
Camborne (see Walk 30), Carn Brea is usually described as the first hill in
Cornwall (for those approaching from the west). It has important histori-
cal associations, and was site of a Neolithic settlement. There are also the
remains of a 13th-century chapel; records from 1396, kept at the County
Records Office, state that 'beaconage' was received from fisherman for the
burning of an 'ecclesiastical light' on the hill. This is the earliest record in
Cornwall of a light being used for navigational purposes. The tradition is
maintained by the Old Cornwall Society, which lights a beacon on Carn
Brea for the summer solstice every year.

Leave the summit by heading south, walking down steep slopes as you descend the ridge to the corner of the open access land. Turn left here and follow the old boundary around the east side of the hill, back to the car park. Retrace your steps onto **Tredinney Common**, and 300m from the road look for a track junction to the left. Follow this northeastwards across the moor, passing to the north side of the china clay works.

CHINA CLAY

China clay (or kaolin, resulting from the partial decomposition of feldspar in granite) was first used in China over 10,000 years ago to make a fine white porcelain. This porcelain eventually made its way into Europe, and was highly prized by the gentry who were at that time still using earthenware pots. A Devonshire apothecary, William Cookworthy, thought there was on obvious gap in the market, and began searching for a local material that resembled the kaolin from China. In 1746 he discovered it on Tregonning Hill near Germoe in Cornwall. It was known locally as moorstone, or growan clay, and Cookworthy worked on a way to improve the purity of the clay, spending 20 years developing his own recipe for 'china clay'.

By the early 19th century Cornish china clay was (and still is) big business, and while the centre of the industry was St Austell, there were small china clay works in various parts of Cornwall, including here on Tredinney Common.

Walk east along the northern boundary of Tredinney Common, and you'll come to a public footpath going north towards **Bartinney Downs** (SW 395 289).

Follow the public footpath across a moor to a junction of paths below the hill of Bartinney Downs and Caer Bran. A short climb to the northwest (left) brings you to the top at 224m, where you'll see the remains of **Bartine Castle**.

Bartine Castle is an Iron Age enclosure. There are lots of prehistoric remains dotted around the hill, including field systems, settlements, tumuli and cairns, and a circular earthwork surrounds the 'castle'. The word 'bartine' comes from the old Cornish word *bretanow*, which means 'fire'. It is thought that the Druids built fires on the top of the hill on the eve of November. Local people would climb the hill to rekindle their own hut fires with those which were consecrated by the Druids.

This whole area is part of two nature reserves managed by the Cornwall Wildlife Trust. Bartinney Nature Reserve lies to the south of the hill, and Caer Bran to the north and east. It's predominantly upland grassland and heath, and is an important site for short-eared owls and wintering hen harriers.

Descend to the east of north to pick up a public footpath, then follow that southeast to a junction through a gate. Follow the path east to gain the byway that you walked out on earlier in the day. Turn left along the byway to get back to your car.

WALK 33
Sennen Cove and Land's End

Start/finish	Sennen Cove: large pay and display car park on Cove Hill (SW 354 263)
Distance	3 miles/4.75km
Total ascent	525ft/160m
Time	2hrs
Terrain	High cliffs; return on heathland paths
Map	OS Explorer 102 Land's End
Nearest town	Penzance

This short walk takes you to Land's End, the most southwesterly point of mainland Britain, from the little village of Sennen Cove. The views back over Whitesand Bay are amazing, while the clifftop walk is one of the finest in the country.

Start by walking west down Cove Hill into **Sennen Cove**. Go behind the lifeboat station and slipway, then do a left

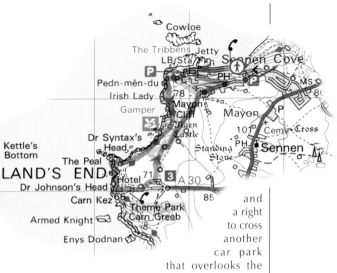

and
a right
to cross
another
car park
that overlooks the
harbour. Pass between two buildings and you'll see a
row of houses ahead. Turn left here, and where the lane
bends to the left you'll see a South West Coast Path signpost pointing to the right. Follow the path southwards
from here.

The path takes you out to the little headland of **Pedn-
mên-du**, and from there southwards again above the
amazing coves and cliffs of Castle Zawn and Gamper.
You'll pass above the Iron Age site of **Maen Castle**.

Maen Castle is an Iron Age promontory or cliff
castle. The castle ramparts are in the form of
a stone wall and ditch built across the neck of a
narrow headland. Maen Castle is one of only two
sites in Cornwall where early Iron Age pottery has
been found, during excavations here in 1939 and
1948–9. In total about 300 pieces of pottery were
found. Some archaeologists believe that the site
was occupied before the fort and its defences were
constructed.

The view along the spectacular granite coast at Land's End

Dr Syntax's Head is a literary reference; just south of Land's End there is Dr Johnson's Head.

Continue around the cliff top to the obvious peninsula of **Dr Syntax's Head**, overlooking the tiny island of The Peal. ◄

The rocky islands of Carn Brâs and the lighthouse of Longships are in view throughout the walk. The original **Longships lighthouse** was built in 1795. The lantern was occasionally obscured by high seas, even though it stood 79ft (24m) above sea level! In 1869 Trinity House began building a new lighthouse out of local granite on Carn Brâs, and the tower was first lit in December 1873. It cost nearly £44,000 to build, but that didn't stop the *SS Bluejack* being wrecked there on a clear night in 1898, and nearly demolishing the structure.

The lighthouse has been unmanned since 1988, and the lantern has a range of 11 nautical miles. Seaward flashes are white, but turn red if any vessels are viewing it from a position close to either Cape Cornwall or Gwennap Head. There is also a foghorn on the rocks, which sounds every 10 seconds.

Just south of Dr Syntax's Head is the hotel and theme park of **Land's End**. Most walkers take photos of the view (and of themselves) then carry on along their route.

We leave the South West Coast Path now and head inland towards the A30 and the large car park on the north side of the access road. On the north side of the car park you'll find a path running along the edge of the open access land. It takes you behind a big white house to where a public footpath leads north with a fence to the right. The path is obvious and leads between heathland (on the seaward side) and grassland back to Sennen Cove.

Pass the first few houses of the village to reach a junction of roads and tracks. Go straight ahead into Maria's Lane, and follow it northeastwards until you come to a lane on your left (by a house on the right called Pol-an-Dre). Turn left down this (Stone Chair Lane), to gain the lifeboat station in Sennen Cove. The road along the shore leads back to your car on Cove Hill.

WALK 34
Around Gwennap Head and Porthcurno

Start/finish	Porthcurno Telegraph Museum car park: pay and display, toilets (SW 384 225)
Distance	5¾ miles/9.25km
Total ascent	1040ft/315m
Time	3–4hrs
Terrain	High cliffs: return through fields (route finding tricky after Raftra Farm)
Map	OS Explorer 102 Land's End
Nearest town	Penzance

This is a great walk around the spectacular coast at Gwennap Head to the promontory fort at Carn Lês Beol. It might be possible to time your visit so that you can enjoy the walk then take in a show at the superb open-air Minack Theatre which is just above the shore in Porthcurno.

Start the walk by heading out of the car park along a path that takes you down through scrub to the lovely white sands of the beach at **Porthcurno**.

The South West Coast Path can be followed to the west side of the beach, taking you above the Minack Theatre and into the car park. Cross the car park to the west side and you'll find the continuation of the path. Walk westwards to the promontory of **Pedn-mên-an-mere**, then above the next gorgeous beach, Porth Chapel.

The path stays close to the clifftops throughout as you head west, first around the headland of Carn Barges, then **Carn Scathe**, and into the narrow inlet at **Porthgwarra**. ◀

Climb steeply out of Porthgwarra on the west side of the cove, rising steeply along the South West Coast Path as you gain the top of **Hella Point**. To the west is **Gwennap Head**, your next destination.

You will find Porthgwarra a much quieter place after the hustle and bustle of Porthcurno, but there are a few houses, a shop, car park and public toilets.

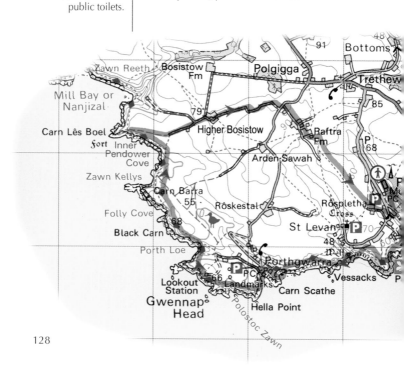

The view at Gwennap Head, showing the amazing granite cliffs

Gwennap Head is the most southerly headland in the Penwith district of Cornwall. It's a popular place with walkers and rock climbers too, with the stunning cliffs of Chair Ladder. It's also a coastal lookout point, and you'll see a pair of navigation markers on the headland, which are in line with the Runnelstone Buoy. The idea is that if the black-and-white marker becomes obstructed by the red marker when viewed from out at sea then the vessel is too close to the Runnel Stone.

The name Gwennap Head is from the old Cornish *Toll Pedn Pennwydh*, which means the 'Holed Head of Penwith'.

Walk round the spectacular headland. The main path does not take you to the blowhole that gives the headland its name, so look for it on the seaward side before you reach the lookout station (there is a faint path leading to it). From the blowhole continue past the lookout station and around above the next big bay, **Porth Loe**.

The route continues close to the clifftops to **Carn Barra**, passing the stunning Folly Cove, then takes you around to Zawn Kellys and Pendower Coves before you reach Higher Bosistow Cliff and the Carn Lês Boel fort.

> This is an ancient monument on the headland above the tiny island of **Carn Lês Boel**. It is marked on the OS map as a fort, but there is some doubt about whether the earthworks and ditch have been correctly interpreted. Some believe that they may be part of an ancient enclosure.

It's now time to return to Porthcurno, and you should walk inland from **Carn Lês Boel**, heading eastwards along a bridleway that takes you initially across the coastal heath, then along an old walled-in, overgrown lane to a house. The track is obvious, and bends round to the farm at **Higher Bosistow**.

As you approach Higher Bosistow turn right in front of the house, following the track around to the east of the house, then between barns. Continue walking generally eastwards on the track between fields, around a few left and right bends, and out to a tarmac lane (SW 373 234). Turn left here, then right in just a few metres, following the bridleway southeast to **Raftra Farm**. Stay on the main track passing a number of cottages and farm buildings, right through to the big barns and a bit of a dumping ground at the southern end of the farm.

Here follow the path around the south side of the barns, heading east. At a corner below the big barn you'll meet another public footpath coming in, and you should turn right. The public footpath runs between fields and can be a bit hard to follow in places. It goes southeastwards directly to the farm at **Rospletha**. To start go to the right of farm buildings at Raftra Farm, then right along an old green lane between hedges. ◀ After two fields on the left of the lane, emerge into the corner of a third field, still going southeast. Turn left at the end of the field, then right again into the next field. The path is now more obvious to Rospletha; when you get there go right for a few metres,

The public right of way is marked on the OS map as being through the fields, but the green lane is the one people use.

then into the farmyard. Cross to the right of the main house and follow the public bridleway to the public road in **Porthcurno** above the Minack Theatre. Turn left and follow the road back to the car park by the Telegraph Museum.

Porthcurno has a unique historic provenance: this is where the undersea telegraph cables that linked Britain with its Empire and other nations came ashore. The valley was the hub of **international cable communications** from 1870–1970 and also home to the training college for the communications industry until 1993. Porthcurno was the largest cable station in the world. There is an interesting museum here which is well worth visiting.

WALK 35
*Lamorna Cove and Valley
from Mousehole*

Start/finish	Mousehole: car park on The Parade, pay and display, toilets (SW 471 265)
Distance	5 miles/8km
Total ascent	810ft/245m
Time	3hrs
Terrain	Undulating coast path; easier return via field paths, often muddy
Map	OS Explorer 102 Land's End
Nearest town	Penzance

A walk along the coast from the picturesque village of Mousehole to beautiful Lamorna Cove, with a return through clifftop fields and along farm tracks.

Start this walk by following the South West Coast Path into the centre of Mousehole, along The Parade and Parade Hill, and turn left along the road to the shore.

Here the South West Coast Path continues to the southwest, high above the shore, and you should follow this throughout.

Walk along the harbour wall, onto North Cliff and South Cliff, then continue along Grenfell Street. Take a right onto Mill Lane, then left along Chapel Street. Chapel Street becomes Raginnis Hill and you should follow this to a junction above the terraces of **Point Spaniard**. ◄

At a Word War II pillbox, another public footpath contours around the slopes, but stick doggedly to the South West Coast Path as it goes down towards the shore through the ancient field systems above **Penzer Point**. Here you'll enter the Kemyel Crease Nature Reserve.

Kemyel Crease Nature Reserve is managed by the Cornwall Wildlife Trust. The reserve is very much a man-made landscape, originally planted with Monterey pine and cypress. These two salt-tolerant species have become very much a part of the local flora.

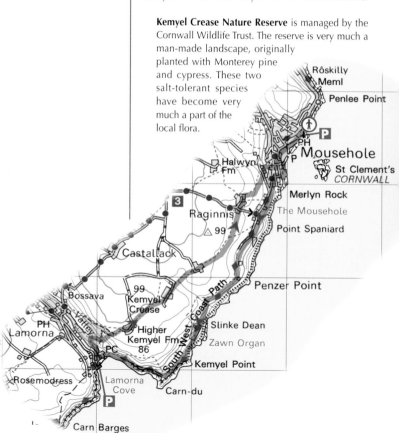

Continue along the coast path, above **Kemyel Point**, climbing slightly to the prominent headland of **Carn-du** at the entrance to Lamorna Cove. The route down into **Lamorna Cove** is a gorgeous walk, and is easy to follow as you approach the bouldery little bay and quay.

Lamorna has been the subject of a number of novels, and has also featured in film and a folk song. During the late 19th century it became a popular retreat for artists of the Newlyn School, and is particularly associated with the artist S J 'Lamorna' Birch who lived there from 1908. There is now an annual Lamorna Arts Festival which began in 2009 to celebrate the original Lamorna Colony, as well as work by the modern art community in the area.

Granite from Lamorna Cove was widely used in construction, not only in the city of London but also in the imposing local landmark of St Buryan's Church.

The return path out of Lamorna Cove is quite steep at first. Start from the car park overlooking the cove and

The beautiful setting of Lamorna Cove, from where granite was taken to build London's Embankment

walk in front of the row of cottages to cross the stream. An obvious footpath climbs up the steep slopes east of the stream in long zigzags, and you soon emerge from the trees on the hilltop at **Higher Kemyel Farm**. Veer right around the cottage and main farmhouse, then follow the very clear track running northeast.

Where the track turns to the left, look for a public footpath sign on the right. This path continues in a northeasterly direction across fields. Cross three fields via two gates to reach **Kemyel Crease Farm**. As you approach the farm don't follow the animal tracks to the left of the farm, but aim across the field to the top right corner, keeping the buildings to your left. You'll emerge onto a lane.

Head north through the farm buildings, and you'll soon approach a sharp bend to the left. Just before this there is a public footpath on the right that leads into a small area of woodland scrub. Take this. Cross a stream, then keep close to the woodland edge to your left, to the easternmost corner. Now follow the path out to the farm at Kemyel Drea.

The OS map shows the public footpath as continuing to the northeast by cutting right through the farm buildings; you will see that there is a narrow gap between the barns, with a clearly marked footpath accessed through a small gateway. Follow this easily, and continue with the field boundary to the left throughout. You soon reach a public footpath junction, with one path making for the coast above Point Spaniard, and the other going north towards Raginnis. Take this latter one to reach the lane at **Raginnis**. The public footpath goes to the left of the cottage as you approach.

Turn right along the lane, then left almost immediately down a track on front of a cottage. Walk along the track then keep to the right of the old derelict buildings at the end, following a public footpath diagonally downhill to the northeast to reach **Mousehole** on Love Lane. Turn left along Love Lane, taking the first right to get back to the harbour side and retrace your outward route back to the car park.

THE LIZARD AND ROSELAND PENINSULAS

The view across Porthbeor Beach towards Zone Point (Walk 39)

WALK 36
Porthleven and Trewavas Head

Start/finish	Porthleven: Kittos Field pay and display car park, behind Porthleven Supermarket (SW 628 259)
Distance	5¾ miles/9.25km
Total ascent	1050ft/320m
Time	4hrs
Terrain	Rough paths and high cliffs; easier return through fields and quiet lanes
Map	OS Explorer 102 Land's End and 103 The Lizard
Nearest town	Helston

A great way to blow away the cobwebs. The route takes you from the wonderful little harbour at Porthleven westwards along the clifftops to Trewavas Head.

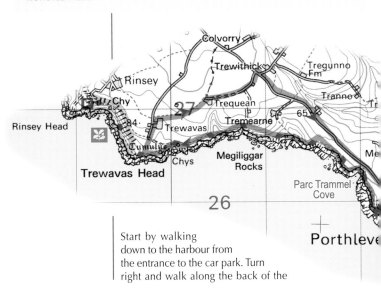

Start by walking
down to the harbour from
the entrance to the car park. Turn
right and walk along the back of the

harbour wall. Turn left and keep along the harbour wall, continuing on to Mount Pleasant Road. ▶

As Mount Pleasant Road bends around to meet Beacon Road you come to a junction. Turn left here into Ocean View, and walk to its end. The path that continues is the South West Coast Path.

> The **South West Coast Path** is a National Trail that takes in the entire southwest of England, starting at Minehead in Somerset on the edge of Exmoor then following the coastline of Devon and Cornwall to finish at Poole Harbour in Dorset. It's 630 miles in total, and has been voted by *Walk* magazine readers (the magazine of the Ramblers Association) as 'Britain's Best Walking Route'.

Pass a monument on the clifftop just along from Ocean View, 'erected in the memory of the many mariners drowned on this part of the coast from time immemorial and buried on the cliffs hereabout. Also to commemorate the passing of the "gryll's" act of 1808 since when bodies cast up by the sea have been laid to rest in the nearest consecrated ground.'

Continue walking westwards around the top of Bullion Cliff, enjoying the views down to the lovely beach in **Parc Trammel Cove**. The going is easy here, and the path is obvious as you approach Tremearne Cliff below the farm of the same name.

Continue along the clifftop path, with a descent into the deep gully at **Trequean**, and a steep climb out the other side.

You're getting nearer to **Trewavas Head** now, and the views along the coast are fabulous. Pass the ruined chimneys of the Trewavas Copper Mine shortly before getting to the headland.

Sitting on the clifftop to the east of Trewavas Head are the two engine houses that form the remains of **Wheal Trewavas mine**. The operation

Look for seals in the water; at high tide you sometimes see harbour porpoise quite close in to the shore here.

137

ran between 1834 and 1846 and was a moderately successful mine employing around 160 men and bringing up around 17,500 tons of copper ore valued at over £100,000. The mine was eventually flooded and abandoned, likely because the diminishing yield rendered it unviable. Because of the way the engine houses cling to the cliff side their seaward walls are significantly taller to compensate for the slope.

From Trewavas Head go inland now to Trewavas Farm. Walk along the track with the farm to your right, and continue until you are just beyond it. Take the public footpath that goes east across fields to **Trequean**. The start of the path is well signposted. As you approach Trequean keep to the left of the farm and you'll come to a couple of tracks. Go down the one to the right, keeping close by the farm buildings. This is the main access road to the farm, and it is easy to follow as you head roughly eastwards to Troon Tanner and the public road near **Trewithick**.

The view across the harbour in Porthleven

138

The walk now follows the public road all the way back to Porthleven. It's a quiet country lane and shouldn't have much traffic along it. As you approach **Porthleven** you'll be on Beacon Road, so can retrace your steps down along Mount Pleasant Road and back to your car.

WALK 37
Halzephron Cliffs from Cury

Start/finish	Car park overlooking Poldhu Cove at the bottom of the hill between Mullion and Cury (SW 667 199)
Distance	3½ miles/5.5km
Total ascent	610ft/185m
Time	2hrs
Terrain	Clifftop path, sandy cove, quiet lane and golf course
Map	OS Explorer 103 The Lizard
Nearest town	Helston

A short walk along the coastal path to a fine old church, then out to the impressive headland at Halzephron Cliff.

Start by heading for the beach. Poldhu Cove is a lovely place to while away the hours, so bring a picnic and enjoy a lazy time down there either before or after you've done this walk. On the north side of the cove there is a dead-end lane. Follow this for a short way until you can pick up the South West Coast Path on the left. The path is easy to follow, and leads around the headland and down into stunning **Church Cove**.

Above Church Cove is the **church of St Winwaloe**. The current building was built in the 14th and 15th centuries, but the tower is a little older. The village of Gunwalloe, for which St Winwaloe is the

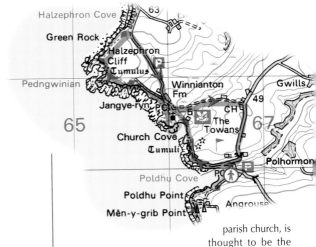

parish church, is thought to be the first entry in the Domesday Book, as the King's Manor at Winnianton is the very first entry for Cornwall.

Climb up from Church Cove to see St Winwaloe's Church, then walk northwest towards the buildings at **Winnianton Farm** and a car park (toilets). Bear left along the South West Coast Path and follow it out to the low headland of **Halzephron**. Continue walking around the headland and you'll reach a minor road (it connects the village of Gunwalloe with St Winwaloe's Church). Turn right along the lane and walk back to the church. As you pass the car park and pass the farm, take the next left and follow a good track up the hill and across the golf course to Towan Cottages. Here you emerge onto the road coming down from the village of Cury. Turn right along the road and follow it down to **Poldhu Cove** and your car.

WALK 38
Mullion Cove and Predannack Head

Start/finish	Car park at Higher Predannack Wollas Farm; follow Ghost Hill on the left as you approach Mullion Cove from Mullion, and drive to the end of the lane (SW 669 162)
Distance	3¾ miles/6km
Total ascent	730ft/220m
Time	2hrs
Terrain	Exposed and high cliffs, one steep ascent; return on good track across heathland
Map	OS Explorer 103 The Lizard
Nearest town	Helston

A superb clifftop route giving the walker great views along the coast, with the possibility of seeing lots of seabirds along the way.

Head along the track from the car park, going east down into a little gully where you cross a stream. Climb out of the other side and you'll come to a path junction. Go right here, cutting across the hill to Lower Predannock Cliff. Here you join the South West Coast Path and should turn right, heading westwards downhill into the bottom of the gully you crossed higher up.

Continue around the spectacular headland to **Predannack Head**, then northwards to **Mên-te-heul**. Here the scenery gets even more amazing, if that is possible. ▶ Beyond Mên-te-heul the paths dips into another stream gully, but the climb out onto **Mullion Cliff** is fairly short.

The land to your right above Mullion Cliff is part of the **Lizard National Nature Reserve**. The clifftop flora is breathtaking in the spring and early summer, and this supports a range of interesting butterfly species,

Offshore the two islets of Mullion and Tregwyn provide a grand foreground to the wider view across Mount's Bay to Porthleven and around the coast all the way to St Michael's Mount.

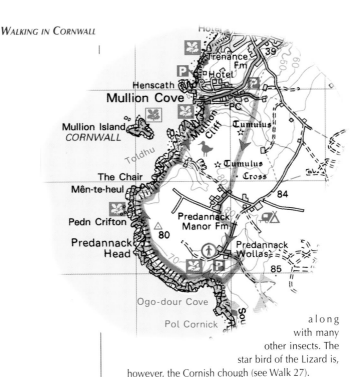

along with many other insects. The star bird of the Lizard is, however, the Cornish chough (see Walk 27).

The little sandy bays of Mullion Cove look stunning down to your left, and as you descend to **Mullion Cove** you really get the feeling that you're stepping back in time as the old fishermen's cottages around the narrow harbour come in to view.

In the late 19th century the **pilchard industry** here had almost collapsed following a few consecutive bad seasons, and many fishermen were either turning their backs on the sea or taking their boats elsewhere. Lord Robartes of Lanhydrock, near Bodmin, persuaded them to stay and to keep trying by financing and building a new harbour. The two new sea walls added to the natural protection

afforded by Mullion Island, and made life here for the fisherman a much safer prospect. The harbour and Mullion Island were donated to the National Trust in 1945 by the Meyer family.

The superb improved natural harbour at Mullion Cove, with Mullion Island offshore

Once down in Mullion Cove walk up the valley (public toilets here) and look for a public footpath on the right that climbs eastwards above where two streams meet. (The footpath starts as a track beside a low barn, next to the last telegraph pole as you head out of the village.)

Follow the track up the hill until you reach a junction at the top. Turn right here. The path initially takes you between a couple of fields, then out onto the wonderful heathland of the National Nature Reserve.

The rock on the Lizard is **serpentine**, which supports a specific flora and fauna. The only other place in the UK that you will find serpentine is right at the very northern tip of the Shetland Islands, on the island of Unst.

143

Follow the public footpath all the way back out into arable land, passing the remains of an ancient cross before you reach a minor road at a bend. Go straight ahead here to **Predannack Manor Farm**. As you approach the farm a public footpath takes you left around the farm buildings. Walk alongside two fields, then turn sharp left across the field and out to the minor lane just along from **Predannack Wollas** where you are parked. Turn right to get back to your car.

WALK 39
Around the Lizard from Cadgwith

Start/finish	Cadgwith: pay and display car park on New Road on the way into the village (SW 719 147)
Distance	6½ miles/10.5km
Total ascent	1200ft/365m
Time	4hrs
Terrain	High cliffs, return along field paths and tracks, muddy in places
Map	OS Explorer 103 The Lizard
Nearest town	Helston

Lizard Point, contrary to popular belief, is the most southerly point in mainland Britain. It's an amazing headland to walk around. It is curious that so many people have this fascination with travelling from Land's End to John o' Groats (John o' Groats isn't the most northerly point in mainland Britain either!). Surely The Lizard to Dunnet Head in Caithness is the natural challenge?

Start by walking down New Road through Cadgwith village towards the coast. Follow New Road around a right-hand bend, then look for Prazegooth Lane on the left. Walk up the lane. At the first sharp bend to the right you'll see the South West Coast Path heading off to the left. Follow the path

LIZARD

through wooded slopes and up to pass between a few houses. Take a left, keeping on the coast path, and you'll emerge above the spectacular blowhole known as **The Devil's Frying Pan**.

Continue walking to the southwest along the coast path. The scenery is spectacular all along here, and you'll pass above high cliffs riddled with caves. The route is obvious throughout. You'll reach **Church Cove**, which is the hamlet just east of Lizard village. There are some old fishermen's cottages here that are absolutely lovely.

Walk around Church Cove then continue along the South West Coast Path to the headland called **Hot Point**. The views from here to Bass Point with

145

The 'new' lighthouse on The Lizard, the most southerly in the UK

The view across the beckoning sands of Housel Cove is backed by the high cliffs and lighthouse of The Lizard.

its lookout station are superb, and you'll soon find yourself striding along the clifftops above **Housel Bay**. ◄

Climb up out of Housel Cove and continue on the coast path to the rocky spur of **Bumble Rock**, then around to the lighthouse at the Lizard.

> The name 'Lizard' comes from the Cornish word *lysardh* which means 'high court'. At 49° 57' 30" North, it is the most southerly part of the British mainland. Only parts of the Isles of Scilly are further south.
>
> The **lighthouse** at the Lizard can be traced back as far as 1619. That original light was extinguished in 1630 due to lack of funds, and in 1751 the

'new' lighthouse was built. It consists of a row of cottages with a tower at each end. Originally both towers would have been lit, but since 1903 only the eastern tower has been used. Trinity House has managed the lighthouse since 1771, and it became automated in 1998. There is a great little heritage centre here which is worth visiting before you carry on with your walk.

Continue westwards along the coast path for 400m to the road head by a cluster of cottages and shops, high above the jetty in **Polpeor Cove**. Another 300m west along the coast path you'll reach a bridleway heading inland. This is your return route to Lizard and Cadgwith, but first you might want to just walk a little further along the clifftop to **Lizard Point** itself.

Return to the bridleway and head northeast. You'll come to the first house of Lizard village on Penmanner Road. Continue along this road to reach The Square. Go north alongside the car park and turn right into Beacon Terrace. Follow the road around a bend to the left, then

The buildings above Polpeor Cove as seen from the lighthouse

slightly right before bending back left at Cross Common. Turn left at Cross Common and walk northwards to where the road takes a sharp bend left again. On this bend you'll see a public footpath going straight ahead; there's a stile to the right of the gate, and this leads onto a track. Walk along the field margin with the hedge to your right, then in the far corner pass through the gap in the hedge so that you are still walking north, now with the hedge to your left. Make your way along footpath towards **Trethvas Farm**.

As you get close to the farm, you'll come to a track. Cut straight over this to reach another track immediately, which becomes a path heading northeast. Follow the waymarkers around the fields to the lane at **Gwavas Farm**. Turn right along the lane, and follow it through the farm. Continue for 400m to a bend and follow it round to the left. Go round the next bend, to the right, then along to Prazegooth. Turn right at the junction, then left immediately, in front of a collection of barns and garages. The lane ahead is Prazegooth Lane and this leads all the way back to **Cadgwith**.

WALK 40
Zone Point

Start/finish	Car park at Porth Farm, just above Towan Beach (SW 867 329)
Distance	5¾ miles/9.25km
Total ascent	1000ft/305m
Time	3hrs
Terrain	Clifftop then shoreline path; return via field paths and tracks, muddy in places
Map	OS Explorer 105 Falmouth & Mevagissey
Nearest town	Truro (by road), or Falmouth (just across Falmouth Bay)

A lovely walk around the southern tip of the Roseland Peninsula, just across the water from the town of Falmouth.

Start by leaving the car park onto the road and turn left, then right down to the beach along a well-marked track. You'll soon find yourself on lovely **Towan Beach**, and might want to spend time here before continuing with this walk.

Once you've finished paddling gain the clifftop South West Coast Path, heading south. The route is obvious: just keep the sea to your left as you go! You'll soon get to **Killigerran Head**, then **Porthmellin Head**, and turn more westwards as you continue to **Porthbeor Beach**.

Stay on the clifftop path all the way to Drake's Downs and **Zone Point**, then around to the fabulous viewpoint on **St Anthony Head**. ▶

Zone Point is the most southerly point of the Roseland Peninsula.

Around from Zone Point is St Anthony Head, and here is a lighthouse set below the highest point of the headland. It was built by Trinity House in 1835, and marks the entrance to the **Carrick Roads**, one of the biggest estuaries in the world, and the mouth of the River Fal.

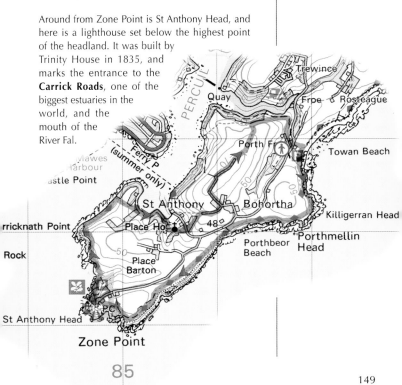

85

On the west side of the highest point of the headland pick up a path that zigzags down to the lighthouse. ◄ Walk back a short way and at a path junction keep left, contouring then descending to a lovely little cove with a white sand beach. Climb back up on the north side of the beach and continue walking to **Carricknath Point**. From here, across the entrance to the Percuil River, you get a great view of St Mawes Castle.

Here you should look out for grey seals in the water.

> **St Mawes Castle** is one of the best preserved of the coastal fortresses built by Henry VIII. It was built to protect the entrance to the Carrick Roads between 1539 and 1545, at a time when there was a real likelihood of invasion by France or Spain. On the west side of the estuary is Pendennis Castle, which was built to serve the same purpose.

The path now takes you northeast and then up and over the little hill of Amsterdam Point into Cellars Beach. Walk down to the shore and follow the path towards impressive **Place House** and the little church at St Anthony.

Go behind the church and house and walk east out to a minor road. Take a right and then a left immediately, following a public footpath sign up the hill with a small wood to your left. Bear right at the top of the hill and walk along a field edge to **Bohortha**.

Go past a postbox hidden in the end of a wall on the right, then turn left along a track by a big open barn. The public footpath soon turns to take you onto the top of the ridge, giving superb views out to the sea to the east and across the river to the west and north. The path is enclosed by hedges all the way and is easy to follow. You will start to descend at the northern end of the ridge to reach a path junction (SW 863 331), with a wooded slope ahead and below. Turn right here, with views over Porth Creek to your left. Follow the path downhill, then at a sharp bend to the right it becomes more of a track and takes you back to the car park at **Porth Farm**.

Walk	Start	Distance	Ascent	Time	Page
Bodmin Moor					
1	Minions SX 259 710	4½ miles/7.25km	525ft/160m	2–3hrs	20
2	near Berriowbridge SX 259 761	4 miles/6.5km	790ft/240m	3hrs	23
3	near Jamaica Inn SX 182 768	6½ miles/10.5km	920ft/280m	4hrs	25
4	Candra SX 117 779	7½ miles/12km	1070ft/325m	5hrs	29
5	near Bowithick SX 183 826	5¾ miles/9.25km	850ft/260m	3.5hrs	33
6	Roughtor car park SX 137 819	4 miles/6.5km	1095ft/335m	3hrs	36
7	Bowthick/Trebray SX 191 826	5 miles/8km	630ft/190m	3hrs	39
The North Coast					
8	Duckpool Beach SS 201 116	7 miles/11.25km	1700ft/520m	4hrs	44
9	Crackington Haven SX 143 967	7¼ miles/11.75km	2030ft/620m	5–5hrs	47
10	Crackington Haven SX 143 967	5 miles/8km	1530ft/475m	3–4hrs	50
11	Boscastle SX 099 912	3½ miles/5.5km	1215ft/370m	2hrs	53
12	Tintagel SX 058 883	3¾ miles/6km	930ft/285m	2–3hrs	57
13	Port Isaac SW 999 809	4 miles/6.5km	980ft/300m	2–3hrs	60

Walk	Start	Distance	Ascent	Time	Page
14	Pentireplaze SW 940 799	3¾ miles/6km	875ft/265m	2–3hrs	63
15	Padstow Harbour SW 918 754	7½ miles/12km	1045ft/320m	4hrs	66
16	Constantine Bay SW 858 745	5¾ miles/9.25km	650ft/200m	3hrs	69
17	Holywell SW 766 587	4¼ miles/6.75km	670ft/205m	2–3hrs	72
18	St Agnes SW 719 504	4½ miles/7.25km	1005ft/305m	3hrs	74
19	North Cliffs SW 625 431	8¼ miles/13.25km	1600ft/490m	5hrs	77
Penwith and West Cornwall					
20	Hayle SW 563 378	5 miles/8km	215ft/65m	2hrs	82
21	Zennor SW 454 384	5¼ miles/8.5km	950ft/290m	3hrs	85
22	Zennor SW 454 384	1¾ miles/2.75km	415ft/125m	1hr	88
23	Treen SW 436 375	3 miles/4.75km	980ft/300m	2hrs	90
24	Bosullow Common SW 418 344	4¼ miles/6.75km	500ft/155m	3hrs	92
25	near Pendeen SW 393 333	2½ miles/4km	190ft/60m	1.5hrs	96
26	Trewellard SW 376 338	4 miles/6.5km	740ft/225m	2.5hrs	98
27	Cape Cornwall SW 353 317	4¼ miles/6.75km	895ft/270m	3hrs	102
28	St Just SW 369 312	3 miles/4.75km	515ft/155m	2hrs	105

Walk	Start	Distance	Ascent	Time	Page
The Inland Mining Districts					
29	Poldark Mine SW 682 314	3¾ miles/6km	305ft/95m	2hrs	110
30	Piece SW 678 397	2¾ miles/4.5km	360ft/110m	2hrs	112
31	Redruth SW 698 421	3 miles/4.75km	240ft/70m	2hrs	115
Land's End					
32	near Sancreed SW 403 297	4½ miles/7.25km	555ft/170m	2–3hrs	120
33	Sennen Cove SW 354 263	3 miles/4.75km	525ft/160m	2hrs	124
34	Porthcurno SW 384 225	5¾ miles/9.25km	1040ft/315m	3–4hrs	127
35	Mousehole SW 471 265	5 miles/8km	810ft/245m	3hrs	131
The Lizard and Roseland Peninsulas					
36	Porthleven SW 628 259	5¾ miles/9.25km	1050ft/320m	4hrs	136
37	Poldhu Cove SW 667 199	3½ miles/5.5km	610ft/185m	2hrs	139
38	near Mullion Cove SW 669 162	3¾ miles/6km	730ft/220m	2hrs	141
39	Cadgwith SW 719 147	6½ miles/10.5km	1200ft/365m	4hrs	144
40	near St Anthony SW 867 329	5¾ miles/9.25km	1000ft/305m	3hrs	148

APPENDIX B
Useful contacts

Tourist information
Visit Cornwall
The official tourist board website.
www.visitcornwall.com
This has links to all the major tourist attractions, accommodation, places to eat, outdoor activities, historical sites, and other things to do during your stay.

The Cornwall Online guide
www.cornwall-online.co.uk
Another useful site to help you plan your holiday.

The National Trust
www.nationaltrust.org.uk
The Trust owns much of the coastal land in Cornwall, as well as a number of historic buildings and other sites of interest.

Transport
Traveline South West
www.travelinesw.com
www.firstgreatwestern.co.uk
Tel: 0345 700 0125
www.nationalrail.co.uk

Other places to visit
The Cornwall Wildlife Trust
www.cornwallwildlifetrust.org.uk
This is the main conservation organisation in the county. The Trust either owns or manages 57 superb nature reserves in Cornwall. They are all worth checking out, and you can download full details of each reserve from their website.

St Michael's Mount
www.stmichaelsmount.co.uk
Tel: 01736 710507
St Michael's Mount (National Trust) should be on everyone's list of places to visit in Cornwall. It is one of the county's most familiar historic sites, and is reached by a causeway which can only be crossed at low tide.

The Lost Gardens of Heligan
www.heligan.com
Tel: 01726 845100
The Lost Gardens are quite rightly one of the chief tourist attractions in Cornwall. The gardens were created by the Tremayne family in the typical 'Gardenesque' style of the 19th century. They became neglected after the First World War but were 'discovered' and renovated in the 1990s.

The Eden Project

www.edenproject.com
Tel: 01726 811911
The other big attraction in Cornwall is the Eden Project, a magnificent collection of plants from around the world, housed in artificial biomes. It is a valuable educational resource, a place for arts and music events, and also a centre of excellence in plant research and conservation.

Cornish Mines

There are countless mines that are well worth visiting in Cornwall. A good starting point for all information relating to the Cornish World Heritage Site is
www.cornish-mining.org.uk.

LISTING OF CICERONE GUIDES

For full information on all our
guides, books and eBooks,
visit our website:
www.cicerone.co.uk

Walking – Trekking – Mountaineering – Climbing – Cycling

Over 40 years, Cicerone have built up an outstanding collection of over 300 guides, inspiring all sorts of amazing adventures.

Every guide comes from extensive exploration and research by our expert authors, all with a passion for their subjects. They are frequently praised, endorsed and used by clubs, instructors and outdoor organisations.

All our titles can now be bought as **e-books**, **ePubs** and **Kindle** files and we also have an online magazine – **Cicerone Extra** – with features to help cyclists, climbers, walkers and trekkers choose their next adventure, at home or abroad.

Our website shows any **new information** we've had in since a book was published. Please do let us know if you find anything has changed, so that we can publish the latest details. On our **website** you'll also find great ideas and lots of detailed information about what's inside every guide and you can buy **individual routes** from many of them online.

It's easy to keep in touch with what's going on at Cicerone by getting our monthly **free e-newsletter**, which is full of offers, competitions, up-to-date information and topical articles. You can subscribe on our home page and also follow us on **Facebook** and **Twitter** or dip into our **blog**.

Cicerone – the very best guides for exploring the world.

CICERONE

Juniper House, Murley Moss, Oxenholme Road, Kendal, Cumbria LA9 7RL
Tel: 015395 62069 info@cicerone.co.uk
www.cicerone.co.uk and **www.cicerone-extra.com**